Twayne's United States Authors Series

Sylvia E. Bowman, *Editor*

INDIANA UNIVERSITY

Mary Wilkins Freeman

MARY WILKINS FREEMAN

By PERRY D. WESTBROOK
State University of New York at Albany

Twayne Publishers, Inc. :: New York

Library of Congress Catalog Card Number: 67-24763

MANUFACTURED IN THE UNITED STATES OF AMERICA BY
UNITED PRINTING SERVICES, INC.
NEW HAVEN, CONNECTICUT

For My Mother
Madeleine D. Westbrook

Preface

THIS STUDY of Mary E. Wilkins Freeman's long and productive literary career is confined to a consideration of her fiction for adults. It is with some regret that I pass over her writing for children, both prose and verse, since much of it is of superior quality. I feel no regret, however, about slighting her poetry for adults, for it is the weakest of all her work.

Critics almost unanimously agree that Mrs. Freeman did her best work before 1900. Not entertaining a dissenting view, I have therefore given her earlier period closer attention, but I have attempted to provide a comprehensive picture of her prolific output after 1900. The majority of this later material, in fact, is by no means totally contemptible, and scattered among it are some of her best pieces.

Mrs. Freeman's greatest strength lies in her insights into the post-Calvinist psyche as it existed in the back-country of New England at the end of the nineteenth century. Accordingly, I have gone to some pains to provide background in the socioeconomic and religious situation of this area during the time when Mrs. Freeman wrote about it. Without such a briefing the reader is likely to lose many of the subtleties in her characterizations and fail to appreciate her important place in the long line of commentators on the Puritan tradition—a line in which, as Paul Elmer More points out, she stands side by side with Nathaniel Hawthorne.

I cannot state strongly enough my gratitude for the patience and skill of the librarians at the State University of New York at Albany in locating for me some of the less obtainable of Mrs. Freeman's works. Especial thanks go to Miss Eleanor Streum and Miss Margaret Wagner. I also thank Dr. Richard Cary of the Colby College Library for his aid and encouragement. To the Research Foundation of the State University of New York I owe a debt of gratitude for a summer research grant which enabled me to gather, in connection with another project, much of the material I have drawn upon in my discussion of beliefs in New England concerning freedom of the will. Finally, to my wife I am deeply grateful for her hours of drudgery in typing and editing my manuscript.

The reader should note that in the title and text of this book I have dispensed with the initial E. (for Eleanor) that Mary E. Wilkins Freeman always included in the name she wrote under both before and after her marriage. In using a less cumbersome form of her name I am following the usual practice among commentators on her work from Henry James to F. O. Matthiessen.

PERRY D. WESTBROOK

State University of New York at Albany

Contents

Chronology

1852 Mary Ella (later changed to Eleanor) Wilkins born in Randolph, Massachusetts, to Warren Wilkins, carpenter, and Eleanor Lothrop Wilkins.
1859 Mary Wilkins starts school. Her sister Anna is born.
1867 The Wilkins family moves to Brattleboro, Vermont, where Mary enters high school.
1870 Mary graduates from high school; enters Mt. Holyoke Seminary in autumn.
1871 Leaves Mt. Holyoke because of ill health; takes courses at Glenwood Seminary, West Brattleboro.
1873 Meets Hanson Tyler, for whom she entertains romantic feelings throughout her life; attempts, unsuccessfully, to teach at a girls' school; Mr. Wilkins' business fails, and he returns to carpentry.
1876 Anna dies.
1880 Mother dies.
1881 *Wide Awake*, a magazine for children, accepts her ballad "The Beggar Kind"; places other poems in the same periodical and in *St. Nicholas.*
1882 Receives fifty dollars from the Boston *Sunday Budget* for her first adult story, "The Shadow Family."
1883 Her father dies while in Gainesville, Florida, on a construction job.
1884 *Harper's New Monthly* accepts her story "A Humble Romance"; returns to Randolph to live.
1885 Trip to New York City and Brooklyn.
1887 Harper publishes *A Humble Romance and Other Stories.*
1891 *A New England Nun and Other Stories.*
1892 Meets her future husband, Dr. Charles Freeman, in Metuchen, New Jersey.
1893 *Jane Field; Giles Corey, Yeoman: A Play.*
1894 *Pembroke.*
1895 *The People of Our Neighborhood.*
1896 *Madelon.*
1897 *Jerome: A Poor Man.* Miss Wilkins suffers from bad

health with nervous symptoms; becomes engaged to Dr. Freeman.

1898 *Silence and Other Stories.*

1899 *The Jamesons.*

1900 *The Love of Parson Lord and Other Stories; The Heart's Highway.*

1901 *Understudies; The Portion of Labor.*

1902 Mary E. Wilkins and Dr. Charles Freeman marry at Metuchen on January 1.

1903 *Six Trees; The Wind in the Rosebush and Other Stories of the Supernatural.*

1904 *The Givers.*

1905 *The Debtor.*

1906 *By the Light of the Soul; "Doc" Gordon.*

1907 *The Fair Lavinia and Others.*

1908 Competes in New York *Herald's* transatlantic novel-writing contest, which she wins with *The Shoulders of Atlas*; participates with Howells, Henry James, and others in writing the "cooperative" novel *The Whole Family.*

1909 *The Winning Lady and Others*; Dr. Freeman enters a New York sanitarium because of alcoholism; Mrs. Freeman suffers from onset of deafness.

1912 *The Yates Pride: A Romance; The Butterfly House.*

1914 *The Copy-Cat and Other Stories.*

1917 *An Alabaster Box.*

1918 *Edgewater People.*

1920 Dr. Freeman, now a confirmed alcoholic, is committed to the New Jersey State Hospital for the Insane at Trenton.

1921 Dr. Freeman escapes from the hospital and temporarily resides at home.

1922 Mrs. Freeman is legally separated from her husband.

1923 Dr. Freeman dies, having disinherited his wife. The will is later successfully contested.

1926 On April 23 Mrs. Freeman receives from the American Academy of Letters the William Dean Howells Gold Medal for Fiction; November 10, is elected to membership in the National Institute of Arts and Letters.

1927 *The Best Stories of Mary E. Wilkins*, edited by Henry W. Lanier.

1930 Mrs. Freeman dies in Metuchen, New Jersey.

Mary Wilkins Freeman

CHAPTER 1

A Young Writer in New England

MARY WILKINS FREEMAN is our most truthful recorder in fiction of New England village life. In several volumes of short stories and three or four novels, she has caught the flavor of that life as no other author has; but when she writes on other subjects, she is usually undistinguished. Yet the New England of which she wrote was in the lowest ebb of its cultural history. Only the memories of its old vigor remained. The Civil War, the westward migrations, and industry had drained the countryside of much of its population. The old Calvinist religion had yielded its hold to Unitarianism or to indifference. Swelling numbers of Irish, French-Canadian, and Polish newcomers were successfully competing with the Yankee inhabitants as farmers, diluting the old way of life with different customs and outlooks. But much of the old remained too—especially in the remoter and smaller communities—and still remains, often in happy amalgamation with the new. Of this remnant, persistent even in the face of overwhelming misfortunes, Mary Wilkins Freeman wrote; and in so doing she described the very essence of the New England character, both in its social and individual aspects. But before examining her writing, one must take a close look at the place and times which provided her material.

I *"Daniel Webster addressed 15,000 here"*

An adventurous motorist traveling Route 7 northward from Bennington, Vermont, may turn east from the highway at Arlington—the home town of Dorothy Canfield Fisher—and follow a narrow, rocky road over the main ridge of the Green Mountains to the township of Stratton. After nearly an hour of steep climbing, before reaching Stratton, he will cross the line between Bennington and Windham counties, about midway between the New York and the New Hampshire borders. A few miles farther on he will cross the Long Trail, a wilderness path following the mountain crests from Massachusetts to Canada. A mile or two more, having skirted some beaver ponds that almost inundate the road, he will come upon one of the most impressive evidences of the calamitous decline of rural New England in the last century. There by the roadside is a sign reading: "Daniel Webster addressed 15,000 here." Close by in a meadow now almost overgrown with spruce and alder—all that remains of the broad field that once was the gathering place for such a concourse—a plaque embedded in a granite boulder more durably commemorates the event.

The motorist, it must be understood, will not have passed, since leaving East Arlington, a single homestead where people live the year around. And he would have to travel far down the other side of the pass before finding any dwelling other than a sportsman's shack. This is a lonely and wild area, one of the wildest in New England outside northern Maine. Yet in the Log Cabin and Hard Cider campaign of 1840, Daniel Webster had taken the trouble to travel here and was able to attract from the farms and villages then flourishing up the nearby slopes and valleys a throng more numerous than the population of any Vermont city today with the exception of Burlington and Rutland. Fifty years later, and to the present, even the most golden-tongued orator would have spoken here only to the pines and the chipmunks. For the people vanished a century ago into Civil War graves, westward to the prairies, or down-country to the manufacturing cities. The town of Stratton in the 1960's numbers only a few hundred souls, and none of them lives near the meadow where Webster spoke.

In this same Windham County, in which Stratton is a township, is located Brattleboro, the home of Mary E. Wilkins from the age of fourteen to thirty-one. In Brattleboro she learned the craft of writing, and there and in the adjacent countryside she found the subjects for many of her best stories and novels. Brattleboro was somewhat of an oasis, perhaps, in a surrounding desert of decay. But to live in Windham County in those years closely following the Civil War was to live in the midst of a demoralized and disintegrating society. The physical evidence was everywhere, not only on Stratton Mountain. Indeed the past haunts the hill country of all New England like a spectral army. If the visitor tramps the footpaths or abandoned roads of any of a hundred upland townships, he will find the vestiges of vanished populations—mile after mile of stone walls interlacing century-old forests; isolated cellar holes or whole villages of them with lilac bushes growing alongside and apple trees ungrafted for generations and yielding a fruit as bitter as the disappointment of the settlers who lived and failed here and then moved on; graveyards, fenced perhaps with granite slabs ten feet long but, even so, inadequate to fend off the intruding forest and underbrush—everywhere the tokens but not the actuality of a once thronging, hopeful life.

Historians have compared the settling of the New England hinterland and its subsequent desertion to the swarming of hives of bees. After the Revolution the coastal areas and the larger river valleys of Southern New England had become overpopulated. For a generation the oxcarts lumbered north and northwestward from Massachusetts and Connecticut until every mountain interval and every slope that could be cleared and ploughed or pastured was pre-empted by the hardy, land-hungry Puritan farmers from the south. They hewed down the forest and built sturdy houses and barns and gathered the stones that littered the land and made of them fences a yard or more thick. At the same time, they erected their churches and schools—the two bulwarks of New England civilization.

At first the farming was on a subsistence level with only a small cash income from potash burned from the trees that had to be felled before tillage could begin. Later, sheep, among them the famous Merino breed, were raised and salable quantities of wool were produced. In Vermont the Morgan horse also became profitable to breed; and, for a time, what with horses and sheep, the northern states prospered. But the soil was thin, the climate harsh, the markets difficult of access. Farmers began to sell out and migrate to the West, especially after the opening of the Erie Canal and the building of the railroads. Relatives writing back home or returning for a visit told of the rich, black, stoneless soil of the Corn Belt and the wheatlands. "Why," a relative back from the West would exclaim, "your whole oat crop is less than gleanings we would have in our field in Iowa."

So the hive swarmed again. Townships, settled scarcely fifty years, emptied out. Long before the Civil War, and with accelerated speed after it, rural populations fell to the vanishing point. Houses rotted and collapsed into their cellars. Fields reverted to underbrush and forest. Deer, at one time almost extinct in New England, returned to remain in droves to the present. The farmers who decided to hold on, perhaps because they had the best land, struggled with uncertain markets—horses were supplanted by engines, and wool was undercut by Australian imports—or finally went into dairying or lumbering. Village merchants, deprived of their customers, closed their shops. Poorhouses flourished, and the young people continued to flee from the hills in pursuit of a living that seemed easy when compared to following a plough or scything hay among the boulders of their thin-soiled meadows.

II *"The Terminal Moraine"*

The people who remained after the various migrations are those about whom Mary Wilkins wrote—the people whom Fred Lewis Pattee designated as representing the terminal moraine of New England Puritanism. What manner of people were these who persisted doggedly on the hill farms and villages far up the narrow valleys of the back country? Their fathers and grandfathers, those settlers who had come from the older areas of the older states, were of course Puritan yeomen of the sturdiest and stubbornest religious persuasion. In order to understand their descendants it is worth while to study the character and way of life of one of these pioneers.

One such early migrant to the north country, Seth Hubbell, wrote an account of his removal from Norwalk, Connecticut, on Long Island Sound to the village of Wolcott, Vermont, almost at the Canadian border—a distance of over three hundred miles. In 1788 he reconnoitered the area, discovered suitable land, and made a clearing where he could later settle his family. Leaving his oxen with another homesteader, he returned to Norwalk to fetch his family. Late in February they set forth by oxcart for their new home—Seth, his wife, his five daughters, a horse, and some cows. Some of the way he had to put his own shoulders to the yoke, for one of his oxen had sickened and eventually died. The last part of the trip Seth and his wife and two oldest daughters—the three others remained at a village along the way—traveled on snowshoes, only to discover that they had lost ownership to the clearing and that one of the oxen left there had also died.

Somehow the family survived the first spring and summer until a crop could be harvested. They sold the horse and all but one of the cows in order to buy new land. A sable that Seth was lucky enough to kill provided a pelt that he could trade in a village fifty miles away for a half bushel of seed wheat. A moose acquired from an Indian supplied the food that averted starvation. With an axe and hoe Seth cleared and planted two acres of land without the aid of oxen, which for five years he could not afford to own. Among the innumerable hardships and calamities he had to endure was the loss of his wife and two of his daughters in a great epidemic.

In 1824, thirty-six years after his coming to Wolcott, Seth wrote of his former life as follows. "When I reflect on those past events, the fatigue and toil I had to encounter, the dark scenes I had to pass through, I am struck with wonder and astonishment at the fortitude and presence of mind that I then had to bear up under them."[1] Hubbell's experience, of course, was not unique; tens of thousands in the 1780's and 1790's had endured, and triumphed over, similar hardships. "The stories of strange lives have been whispered to the earth, their thoughts have burned themselves into the cold rocks," wrote Sarah Orne Jewett of the farms and villages founded by men like Seth.[2] Yet by the time Hubbell was writing his memoirs, Wolcott and the rest of the New England hill country had already reached its zenith of population and prosperity. The decline was soon to set in, if it had not already started.

The salient fact about lives like Seth Hubbell's is the incredible will power that underlay their endurance and achievement. Hubbell's own "astonisment" at his accomplishments indicates that he did not give all the credit to himself, that he felt he was drawing on sources of strength outside himself. The Calvinist doctrines of election and of the perseverance of saints must have played a part in helping such persons persist. Among Puritan names Endurance was a favorite because it was a favorite Puritan virtue and a very useful one in the settlement of the wilderness. But only God's chosen ones, those predestined to salvation, can persevere through circumstances that would destroy less favored persons. Man's will and God's predestination are undefeatable when allied, for man's will then becomes an expression of God's. Even after the need for superhuman endurance no longer existed, the individual's trust in the invincibility of his will, when in his opinion it coincided with God's will, lingered. Sometimes this Puritan will power found useful expressions of itself. Sometimes—very frequently in Mary Wilkins Freeman's stories—it exerted itself on ignoble goals, mere whims and eccentricities, with all the force with which it had been directed against the hostile wilderness when its goal was the establishment of the New Jerusalem in New England.

The purpose of Miss Wilkins in her writing was to exhibit these latter-day manifestations of the Calvinist will, just as Ellen Glasgow's was to explore similar vestiges in the characters of the Presbyterian Calvinists of Western Virginia. Miss Glasgow, to be sure, celebrated the more positive aspects: the "vein of iron," the inflexible endurance, that carried her Virginians through the catastrophes of the modern world. Miss Wilkins specialized, though not exclusively, in the almost pathological manifestations of the overdeveloped will deprived of a worthwhile outlet for its powers. Miss Wilkins saw Calvinism as a chaotic deposit of flinty, fruitless irrelevancies. Miss Glasgow saw it as a continuing important influence in American life, always serviceable whether in Indian wars or the Great Depression.

The New England countryside in Miss Wilkins' youth, though catastrophically thinned by the exodus to the West and the factory towns, was not totally drained of its best stock. In certain hard-hit communities, to be sure, shiftlessness and decay and inbreeding were the order. But other villages retained some of their standards along with people of character who strove to perpetuate the tradition of hard work, thrift, and righteousness. The schools and the academies continued to teach the three R's and the classics. The churches continued to preach only a slightly watered-down orthodoxy. Some towns were spending more money on their poorhouses than on their roads, but the struggle to stay out of the poorhouse—not "to go on the town," as the saying was—was added incentive to a parsimonious, hard-working way of life. The aims had become petty when compared to those of the pioneer days, but they were still compelling enough to keep many people of simple character from total moral collapse and to keep more complicated persons from anything worse than oddness. It is doubtless better to be dully moral, or eccentric, than to be degenerate. Wisely Miss Wilkins chose to write about the former types rather than about the degenerates.

But only rarely did she depict a truly noble character rooted in the soil of decayed Calvinism.

III *The New England Town*

To understand Miss Wilkins' best works, one must know the social and political setting of the New England town in which the action occurs. To begin with, there is a remarkable similarity among all New England towns in their physical arrangements, in the ideals they uphold, and in the character traits they nurture. One may choose an island township on the Maine Coast, a Champlain Valley township in Vermont, or a hill township in Connecticut; and one will find that the similarities among them far outnumber the differences.

The town itself is usually comprised of a number of villages, all of which, along with the intervening countryside, are under the same government. The village which contains the town offices is near the center of the township and is the most important in other respects, containing the largest schools, churches, and shops. This central village is generally built at a crossroads, or perhaps around a common or "green." Here, aside from the public buildings, are the residences of the professional men and the shopkeepers. But many of the dwellings are farmhouses, their meadows and pastures extending behind the village streets. Stretching outward are roads to the outlying parts of the township, which might be a hundred square miles in area.

Presiding over the religious, intellectual, and political life of the town are a set of popularly elected or appointed dignitaries. The churches have their pastors and deacons, congregationally chosen, to supervise the spiritual welfare of the citizens through Sunday services and sermons and Thursday evening lectures and prayer meetings. The secular government resides in the town meeting, made up of all voting citizens. Each year, usually in March, the voters meet to discuss community affairs and to delegate their powers to elected administrative officials: a panel of three or five selectmen, who are the general executors of the town laws; a road agent or commissioner, who keeps the public highways passable; a clerk, who records vital statistics and keeps the town records; a town treasurer; a constable; and a variety of other officials, such as an overseer of the poor, a fence-viewer, and a keeper of weights and measures. Lastly the meeting elects a school board to maintain the educational buildings, hire and fire teachers, and administer school finances.

The effects of such a closely knit community organization are obvious. Literally every voter who goes to town meeting has a voice in government. He may speak his mind and cast his vote and, if he wishes, can probably hold an office himself some time during his life. With such universal participation in town affairs the sense of membership becomes strong. Furthermore, through the agency of the churches and the schools, the ideals, the values, and the mores of the group are inculcated early and indelibly into every child. Feelings of security are undoubtedly strengthened by such homogeneity. But also strengthened is a concern for what others think. Since one of the values is self-reliance, an area of inner conflict appears: if one is not independent in thought and action, the community frowns on him; if one's independence leads to a flaunting of other established values, the community frowns. With such conflicts many of Miss Wilkins' stories deal. The conflicts, as will be seen, become very intricate when they occur in a person endowed with a Calvinistically trained conscience and will—a will whose direction is conceived of as revealing one's relation to God and one's chances of salvation.

IV *Randolph, Massachusetts*

Into such a community—Randolph, Massachusetts—Mary E. Wilkins was born on October 31, 1852. Though only fourteen miles from the center of Boston, Randolph was in those days a typical rural New England town. It was, moreover, one of the towns that in the first years of the Republic had peopled the settlements in the northern states of Vermont, New Hampshire, and Maine. Being in an old district of New England, it was prototypal. Closely knit racially and culturally, still church-centered, agricultural right up to its main street, it differed only in that it possessed more industry than the remoter communities. In the 1850's Randolph had produced a million dollars' worth of shoes annually, many of them for the Australian market. The manufacturing was carried on in small factories and in little sheds in the yards of shoemakers' houses on a domestic-industry basis. But the days of domestic crafts were numbered. In the 1860's the Australian market vanished, and the local industry became concentrated in larger mills, notably at nearby Brockton.

By the time Mary Wilkins was twelve years old, Randolph had gone the way of many a small New England mill town, where deserted factories were as common as abandoned farms. In its farming, too, Randolph suffered severely along with the rest of the region, though not so disastrously as the less fertile hill sections.

Mary Wilkins' parents were both natives of Randolph. Her father, Warren Wilkins, was connected on both sides with ancient and honored Salem families. Like Hawthorne, Mary Wilkins numbered among her forebears an ancestor involved in the persecution of witches in the seventeenth century; and in the play *Giles Corey, Yeoman* she wrote of the witchcraft delusion. By trade, Warren Wilkins was a carpenter, a house-builder; he was reputedly an overly conscientious man, sensitive, usually fun-loving and cheerful, but occasionally a victim of somber moods. Mary Wilkins' mother, Eleanor Lothrop by birth, could also trace her descent on both sides from New England settlers of the 1640's. Her father, though a housepainter, was a man of considerable means.

When Mary was born, her parents were living in a new house on South Main Street in Randolph. There had been a previous baby who had died in infancy. Born a few years after Mary was a brother, who died at the age of three. A sister, seven years Mary's junior, survived to the age of seventeen. Not a strong child herself, Mary was naturally the object of the doting care of parents whose children had such a propensity to die. In addition Mary was pretty and winsome and seems to have been somewhat spoiled. Yet the Puritan tradition of rearing children had not so far weakened as to exempt her from a strict code of behavior. Obedience certainly was inculcated in home and school and church, as were the virtues of thrift, honesty, temperance, piety—and whatever else is encompassed in a broad construction of the Decalogue.

The Sabbaths were observed in the Wilkins household with all the old-time rigidity, for both parents were orthodox Congregationalists. The schedule of religious activities engrossed all of Sunday: 10:30 to 12:00, worship and sermon; 12:00 to 1:00, Sunday school; 2:00 to 3:30, a preaching service; 4:00 to 5:00, a young peoples' service; 7:00 to 8:00, prayer meeting. Such a program, attended in its entirety by the faithful and their families, ensured that over the years a child would become thoroughly familiar with the Bible and its Calvinist interpretations, with church dogma, and with the application of Scriptural and doctrinal teachings to the problems of daily living. By adulthood a churchgoer in a New England town of one hundred years ago was well-grounded in practical and theoretical theology. In every family religion was discussed, even among the hired help; and the Wilkins family was no exception. If, as her biographer Edward Foster says, Mary Wilkins when a young child could not understand fully the niceties of doctrine discussed in her hearing, "she must at least have learned that theology in her family was bound up with deep personal feelings and that somehow faith and goodness were related to one's material success in the world. In her house, it was always assumed that the poverty of the poor was punishment for sin."[3]

For the thirty years prior to Mary's birth, the pulpit in the Randolph Congregational church had been occupied by a pastor who preached only a slightly diluted Calvinism. There followed two preachers who were more tainted with liberalism. Most important in Mary's spiritual life was John C. Labaree, who took the pastorate at Randolph in 1865. Though far from a Unitarian, Dr. Labaree preached an orthodoxy largely shorn not only of the terror but of the vigor of Calvinism. Many of the old conceptions were still there—original sin, regeneration and sanctification of the soul through the grace of God operating as the Holy Comforter, justification before God, and remission of sins exclusively through the atonement of Christ. But the pivotal Calvinistic doctrine of election was played down in Dr. Labaree's church; nor was there any harping on, or belief in, the wrathful nature of God in dealing with sinners, the prospect of eternal hellfire for those not chosen for salvation, the necessity of adoring the God that might well have predestined one from before his birth to damnation. This moderate, rather kindly religion, is the one that Mary Wilkins adopted for herself. But she knew also, from her parents and their generation, the old-time religion handed down from the Puritan forefathers.

School probably influenced Mary Wilkins less profoundly or lastingly than did church. Beginning at the age of seven, she attended the common school in Randolph. Grades one to seven were kept by one young woman whose salary was two dollars a week and whose own education had not gone beyond high school. From her Mary learned the three R's but probably little else. Because of frail health she was not permitted to play much with other children, and thus she was denied the opportunities for social development that doubtless are an important by-product of school. Being naturally bright and receiving from her teacher the same deference she was used to at home, she soon earned from her fellow pupils the titles "stuck-up," "teacher's partial," and "little dolly-pinky-rosy."[4] In short, she was accorded the usual treatment experienced by an exceptional child at school: the teacher petted her, and the children hated her. Thrown back on herself, she must have come to value more and more the rewards of self-reliance as well as to understand its pains. In numerous stories she later described the struggles of strong-willed individualists in a disapproving and jeering community. The fact that the protagonist in such stories finds peace of mind only when he returns to the village norm suggests that Mary Wilkins must have suffered from her ostracism, however bravely she may have shrugged it off. Acceptance, after all, is sweeter to most human beings, especially to children, than is rejection.

Not that Mary was totally without playmates. Early in childhood, indeed, she established one friendship that survived until the intervention of death. This friend was Mary Wales, the daughter of a Randolph farmer whose one hundred acres fronted on the main street not far from the school. After classes, the two girls often went to the farmhouse and spent long hours there. Here Mary Wilkins learned about farm life both in the fields and barns and in the housewife's kitchen—knowledge that supplied her with details for countless writings. Much later, Mary lived for fifteen years with the Waleses as a friend and boarder.

Growing up in Randolph made Mary Wilkins a New England village woman, whatever she might become or wherever she might live later. Fixed in her memory as childhood's most indelible impressions were the great elm-shaded houses along Main Street, the school and the church and the faith and culture they preserved, the long snowy winters, the raw bleak springs, the brief simmering summers, and the autumns ablaze with crimson and yellow. Here she gained her knowledge of the lifelong toil of the farmer, the parsimony of the peddlers hawking their pots from door to door, the meanness of village gossip purveyed in whispers in stove-heated kitchens, and the unsung heroism of those who defied gossip to be true to themselves, however queer or even warped their selves might be. Here also she tasted the security of living in a homogeneous community, in which most of one's acquaintances and neighbors were of the same Anglo-Saxon stock, subscribed to the same ancestral credos and codes of behavior, spoke the same dialect of the same language, and knew one another's family histories for generations back. And here she learned of the insecurity that homogeneity can foster—not only fear of what people may think or say, but dread of the complete or partial exclusion that comes with nonconformity, all the timidities that Emerson and Thoreau, themselves New England villagers, strove to exorcise in such essays as "Self-Reliance" and "Civil Disobedience."

V *Brattleboro, Vermont*

Along with softening modifications of religion, the post-Civil War decades brought worsening economic conditions to Randolph as to the rest of non-urban New England. Randolph was in part dependent on farming, and the farmer all over New England was in distress. Shoemaking, the other mainstay of Randolph, was suffering from declining markets and concentration in larger manufacturing centers. The result was a dwindling population and hard times for those who remained. As early as 1867 Warren Wilkins, no longer able to make a good living in Randolph, moved to Brattleboro, Vermont, where he intended to establish a drygoods store with his friend Owen Slate. Though Wilkins had bought a lot in a fashionable residential section of Brattleboro, he established his family in a small cottage near the common until the new house was built. Nearby was the Vermont Insane Asylum, which furnished Mary Wilkins with many a glimpse of personality distortions suggestive of those she later wrote about. Mary, now fifteen, attended the public high school, an excellent one, where she took the usual courses in Latin, natural philosophy, mathematics, and rhetoric. An able student, she contributed to the elocution recitations presented by the students and wrote skits for production at school entertainments.

Brattleboro, a fashionable spa before the Civil War, was still a town with some pretense to cultural importance. Among its many old and honored families were the Tylers, true Brahmins who had produced an impressive roster of jurists and clergymen —and even one man of letters, Royall Tyler. In Mary Wilkins' time the arts were still cultivated, and the life of the mind and the spirit was still nurtured by an active lyceum, a first-rate bookstore, and a well-known orchestra under the direction of Christian Schuster. Among the notable native sons were the sculptor John Larkin Mead, Jr., the painters William Morris Hunt and Robert G. Hardie, and the architect Richard Hunt. In belles-lettres, aside from Mary Wilkins herself, the city could claim the essayist Samuel M. Crothers and, for several years, Rudyard Kipling, who had married a Brattleboro girl, Caroline Balestier, a friend of Mary's. A neighbor was the writer Colonel T. W. Higginson's sister Anna, who presided over a "salon" of the artists and people of culture in the town, though Miss Wilkins was either too timid or proud to force herself into this circle.

In 1870 Mary graduated from the Brattleboro High School and entered Mt. Holyoke Female Seminary, which "combined a thorough intellectual training with careful religious culture."[5] But life there was too rigorous for Mary's health, and she left after a year. One thing that Mt. Holyoke could be counted on doing, as those who know the life of Emily Dickinson will recall, was to arouse the religious sensitivities of its students. Indeed, one of its avowed purposes was to bring to "conversion" every girl who had not previously had that experience. Whether a girl resisted, as did Emily Dickinson, or was already a full church member, as was Miss Wilkins, the hammering away at the collective student conscience at prayer meetings and church services, not to mention the annual revivals, could only intensify whatever religious preoccupations one might have. It was not by chance that many Mt. Holyoke girls became missionaries' wives. Like Emily Dickinson, Mary Wilkins found that a year in this atmosphere was all she could stand. After leaving Mt. Holyoke, she returned to Vermont and spent the following year taking courses at a girls' seminary in West Brattleboro. Thus ended her formal education. Mary was an avid reader, however, though a somewhat haphazard one. She and her closest friend, Evelyn Sawyer of nearby Newfane, read and discussed Goethe, Emerson, Thoreau, Dickens, Thackeray, Poe, Hawthorne, Harriet Beecher Stowe, and Sarah Orne Jewett.

In 1873 Mary met Hanson Tyler, a navy ensign on leave home after a tour of duty in Havana. She fell deeply in love with him, but he did not return her feelings, at least not strongly enough to prompt a proposal of marriage. But, like many an old maid in her stories, Mary cherished her unrequited love through middle age, even after Tyler himself had married. Among her keepsakes were a photograph of him and buttons from his naval uniform.

In the same year, a time of business depression, Warren Wilkins was forced to sell his drygoods business and return to his former trade of carpentry. Long ago he had given up his plan of building a house for his family on the site he had purchased on first coming to Brattleboro. To help financially, Mary tried teaching in a school for girls but quit after a year because she found herself unsuited for the work either by interest or by ability. For a time she thought of becoming an artist, inspired perhaps by the examples of the Hunts and John Larkin Mead, Brattleboro boys who were making a name for themselves in the outer world. But she had little talent for painting; and for want of anything else to do, she began to write, at first mainly poetry, for which she had shown some aptitude as a child. Her initial efforts, religious in theme, she did not offer for publication. A little later she turned to children's verse, some of which she was able to place without pay in an obscure Fall River magazine. Not for years did her writing earn her any money. Yet she had found her interest and proceeded to fill a box with manuscripts and rejection slips.

The years passed as she wrote on unnoticed in the dreamy little city that seemed to be existing, like so much of New England, largely in its past. But the author was not spared the buffets of life. In 1876 came a devastating blow; Mary's sister Anna, who was engaged to one of Christian Schuster's musicians, died at the age of seventeen. With their strong New England attachment to place, the family took the body back to Randolph for burial. Meanwhile, the father's financial position continued to deteriorate, and a change in his living arrangements became necessary. In 1877 the family moved into the household of the ailing Reverend Thomas Pickman Tyler, Hanson Tyler's father, where Mrs. Wilkins was to serve as housekeeper. Many of Mary Wilkins' fictional characters have regarded no greater degree of subserviency than this to be the ultimate disgrace that could befall them. The pride of the Wilkinses, who believed poverty to be punishment for sin, must have been sorely bruised. And for Mary this relationship with the parents of the man she loved must have been hard to bear. However, the Wilkinses remained on terms of social equality with the Tylers in the tradition of rural New England, where servants are always "help" and eat at the table with their employers. With one of the Tylers, Aunt Bessie Tyler Billings, Mary was on terms of close friendship. The two took frequent rides together into the country around Brattleboro, especially up the Connecticut and West River valleys, where the depopulated villages and crumbling, abandoned farmhouses everywhere in evidence cast a gloom on the bright green beauty of the hills. These excursions were providing Mary with the settings, the atmosphere, and the moods which were soon to characterize her best work.

VI *"Faithful, hopeful, and independent work"*

Residence with the Reverend Pickman Tyler ended abruptly with the death of Mrs. Wilkins when she was only fifty-three. The shock was a brutal one to Mary, who had always leaned on her mother's strength. Moving to new quarters, she kept up her morale by keeping house for her father and by continuing her writing. Finally in 1881 she received her first monetary reward for authorship, ten dollars in payment for the ballad "The Beggar King" that she had placed in the children's magazine, *Wide Awake*. The poem runs to some fifty stanzas that tell a story in continuation of the nursery rhyme:

> Hark! Hark! Hark! The dogs do bark!
> The beggars have come to town;
> Some in rags and some in tags,
> And some in velvet gowns.

The poem tells how the Beggar King besieged another king's city and forced the king to marry the Beggar Princess, and how this second king fell in love with the Princess at once and married her without demur. Edward Foster's remarks on the poem are well taken: "Miss Wilkins is completely at home in this metier: she smoothly manages the ballad stanza and its internal rhymes; the story swings along with gusto; the images flash with bright and romantic beauty."[6]

To be able to write first-rate children's verse, especially in the late nineteenth century when many of the best writers for adults tried their hand at juvenile writing, is a creditable accomplishment. Miss Wilkins quickly placed more poems and a three-page story in *Wide Awake*, and in 1882 she began selling to the best of all children's magazines, *St. Nicholas.* Then in January, 1882, with her first adult story, "The Shadow Family," she won a fifty-dollar prize from the Boston *Sunday Budget.* (Unfortunately, no copies of this story either in manuscript or in print have survived.) In September, 1882, *Century* published a poem of hers, "Sweet Phyllis," and the townspeople began to take notice. Ladies who had never before acknowledged her acquaintance became suddenly friendly. She was beginning to enjoy the sweetness of success in addition to a much-needed cash income. From now on, she found a market for as much as she could write.

In the autumn of 1882, Mary's father, in poor health, went to Gainesville, Florida, where he had found employment in construction work. That winter in Brattleboro Mary wrote the first story of those later to be included in her first major book, *A Humble Romance.* This story, "Two Old Lovers," recounts a situation common in the writing of Mary Wilkins and of other New England regionalists—a love affair that prolongs itself from the youth to the old age of the lovers but never culminates in marriage. Miss Wilkins' treatment of the subject is distinctive, however, and presaged her manner in the years to follow. The setting, a decaying New England mill town suggestive of Randolph, is sketched with an accuracy that conveys painfully its stagnation and drabness. The male lover, David Emmons, who is the weaker of the pair, as is usual in Mary Wilkins' stories, is the victim of total atrophy of the will. The story is in fact a study of the workings of the will, or lack of will, in the two main characters—and this theme also is highly representative of Miss Wilkins' work.

David Emmons has simply lacked the will power to propose to his sweetheart, Maria Brewster; and after half a lifetime of indecision he dies without asking the question. Maria all along has displayed excessive patience and devotion that in themselves are abnormalities. As her tongue-tied lover grows older and feebler, she cooks for him. She is by his bedside at his death, when he owns: "Maria, I'm—dyin' an'—I allers meant to—have asked you —to marry me" (36).

Miss Wilkins had sent the manuscript of "Two Old Lovers" to Miss M. L. Booth, editor of *Harper's Bazar.* As soon as Miss Booth saw the handwriting, which resembled that of a child, she decided to reject the story. But glancing at it a little more closely, she became interested in it and after three readings accepted it. The story brought its author twenty-five dollars and a strong sense of accomplishment. Her enthusiasm for writing, now intensified, scarcely slackened for the next forty years. The story was a landmark in her development because it was the first to employ successfully the materials she knew the best—a village like the one in which she had grown up and persons like the ones she had known all her life. "A young writer," she advised many years later, "should follow the safe course of writing only about those subjects she knows thoroughly, and concerning which she trusts her own convictions. . . . She should make her own patterns and found her own school. . . . The keynote of the whole is, as in every undertaking in this world, faithful, hopeful, and independent work."[7]

But Mary's joy at the *Harper's Bazar* acceptance was soon dampened. A few months later word came that her father had died in Florida. Burial was in the family plot in Randolph, where her sister and now both her parents had been laid to rest within only six years. Like so many spinsters in her fiction, she was left alone with only her beloved yellow cat Augusta. After the interment she returned to Brattleboro, remaining there with her friends until the end of the year. *Harper's Bazar* in the meanwhile published three more stories. Christmas she spent in Randolph, where in the following summer she took up permanent residence with her former playmate Mary John Wales in the old farmhouse she had known so well as a child.

Though she often returned to Brattleboro on visits, she never made her home there again. Yet the Brattleboro years left an indelible mark upon her as a person and as an artist. It was the place where she had received her schooling, where she had achieved her first successes, where she had experienced her first and probably most deeply felt love for a man, where her sister and mother had died, and where she had last lived with her father. A careful reading of her early stories and novels reveals that by far the larger proportion of them have Vermont settings, not so much Brattleboro but the surrounding countryside in Windham County. The characters, too, in the writing of this period, with their taciturnity, their fierce independence, and their self-will are more suggestive of Vermont than of the Massachusetts seaboard. Yet beyond being strictly New England, Miss

Wilkins' stories are not for the most part closely localized. She knew both the Massachusetts and the Vermont villagers and country people, and she found the likenesses between the two to be much more noticeable than the differences. Later, as the immediacy of her Vermont years wore off, she drifted more into settings reminiscent of Randolph, but the people she wrote about remained much the same. Miss Wilkins knew New England from deep involvement in two of its states, and in most of her writing there is an amalgam of her knowledge of each.

CHAPTER 2

A Humble Romance

IN 1883 Mary Wilkins published her first book, a little volume of poems for children entitled *Decorative Plaques*, with "designs" by George F. Barnes. As a poet, Miss Wilkins is negligible, though she had a knack for lively, rollicking children's verse. Her more important serious efforts, though a selection of them found their way into various verse anthologies, are facile not only in their meter but also in their sentiments. They add nothing to Miss Wilkins' reputation.

There followed two volumes of stories for children: *The Cow with the Golden Horns and Other Stories* (1884) and *The Adventures of Anne: Stories of Colonial Times* (1886), a collection of pieces previously published in *Wide Awake*. Competent though she was in telling tales for young people, Miss Wilkins' work in this genre, which is represented by an occasional volume throughout her career, need not concern the student. None of these works are read today, mainly because she created in them no compellingly lifelike characters—as did her contemporaries Mark Twain, Thomas Bailey Aldrich, and Louisa May Alcott in their books for boys and girls. Classics for children are even rarer than those for adults.

I *"And* they *are American"*

By 1887 the stories Miss Wilkins had written for *Harper's New Monthly* and for *Harper's Bazar* were collected in a volume of over four hundred pages entitled *A Humble Romance and Other Stories.* One of her most successful and enduring books, it contains a half dozen or so stories that she never surpassed either in narrative skill or in psychological insight. In the entire volume she confined herself exclusively to the material which she knew the best: the life and people of the New England village. For an Edinburgh Edition of the first fourteen selections in *A*

Humble Romance, Miss Wilkins wrote in 1889 a brief Preface stating her purpose. Since this is one of the very few comments on her own work that she ever wrote and since copies of the Edinburgh Edition are very difficult to find even in our larger libraries, her remarks deserve to be quoted in full:

> These little stories were written about the village people of New England. They are studies of the descendants of the Massachusetts Bay colonists, in whom can still be seen traces of those features of will and conscience, so strong as to be almost exaggerations and deformities, which characterised their ancestors.
>
> These traces are, however, more evident among the older people; among the younger, they are dimmer and more modified. It therefore seems better worth the while to try to preserve in literature still more of this old and probably disappearing type of New England character, although it has been done with the best results by other American authors.
>
> I hope these studies of the serious and self-restrained New England villagers may perhaps give the people of Old England a kindly interest in them, and I have accepted with pleasure the proposal of Mr. Douglas to include the *Humble Romance* in his "Series of American Authors."

The setting of the stories in *A Humble Romance*, the greater number of which Miss Wilkins wrote either in Brattleboro or a year or so after leaving it, is predominantly Vermont. The stories are developed in an atmosphere of decay common to most New England villages. She had become an important interpreter of New England life under conditions of decline; her fiction was later cited in sociological articles. Rollin Lynde Hartt, for example, in a two-part study published in the *Atlantic Monthly* in April and May in 1899 under the title of "A New England Hill Town" gave her the status of an authority. The articles are not only a testimony to Miss Wilkins' accuracy as a reporter, but they give interesting factual insights into the milieu that she had made her specialty.

The town that Mr. Hartt describes is in the hills of Western Massachusetts, a region closely similar to the Southern Green Mountains where Miss Wilkins had lived. "The rural environment," Hartt writes, "is psychically extravagant. It tends to extremes. A man carries himself out to his logical conclusions; he becomes a concentrated essence of himself" (564). Inbreeding, he finds, creates exaggerated types: misers, hermits, and a great assortment of other eccentrics, as well as mental and physical defectives. The hill towns are anachronisms, despite the efforts of older people to keep them alive. They are communities without hope, harboring the ambitionless and the children of the ambitionless. Most deplorable and ruinous is the absence of contact with the outside world. In families from which a child has gone to college or in which a city person has been welcomed, vitality returns—which would indicate that, like Miss Wilkins, Hartt considers the chief shortcomings of these towns to be cultural rather than eugenic, despite his references to inbreeding. At any rate, of all those who have attempted to depict life in these forgotten towns, Hartt considers that Mary Wilkins has been far and away the most true to life. Appearing in featured articles in New England's leading periodical, such praise is not to be undervalued.

The writers and the social scientists were in accord in their treatment of rural New England. In *Something About Myself,* Rudyard Kipling, who lived in Brattleboro during the 1890's and who perhaps knew Mary Wilkins' stories though he does not cite them, writes in an even darker vein than does Hartt: "The country was large-boned, mountainous, wooded, and divided into farms of from fifty to two hundred barren acres. Roads, sketched in dirt, connected white clap-boarded farmhouses, where the older members of the families made shift to hold down the eating mortgages. The younger folk had gone elsewhere. There were many abandoned houses too; some decaying where they stood; others already reduced to a stone chimney-stack or mere green dimples still held by an undefeated lilac bush" (118-19). He speaks of the taciturnity, the suspiciousness of the New England country folk, who accepted him only because his wife was a Vermonter. The lives lived on these farms were lonely and sterile: "What might have become characters, powers, and attributes perverted themselves in that desolation as cankered trees throw out branches akimbo, and strange faiths and cruelties, born of solitude to the edge of insanity, flourished like lichen on sick bark" (127).

As in Miss Wilkins' stories, the females were in the ascendancy in this society, but they imparted to it few feminine graces. The men, Kipling observed, were ruled from babyhood and through school by strong-willed, acid-tongued women, often spinsters; when the men reached marriage, they were often terrified of the opposite sex. A man was obliged to drink on the sly (and still is in rural New England) to avoid the wrath of his wife, sister, or mother. Consequently, obsessive drinking was common, as so often is the case when alcohol is prohibited. On the farms especially, men would become maniacally drunk on hard cider. Slowly, as the old stock died out, immigrants—"the wreckage of Eastern Europe"—moved in, or city people took over the farms for vacationing. The natives hated and resented both intruders.

Yet—and this is important—Kipling had feelings other than pity or condemnation for the Vermont farmers. In a dispatch from Brattleboro to the London *Times*, November 29, 1892, he pictures them as superior to the distraught city people who flock into the countryside each summer to recuperate from the ravages of their hectic living during the rest of the year—people who will never achieve the steadfastness, the repose, and the purposefulness of their rustic neighbors.

> Down in the meadow the mowing machine has checked, and the horses are shaking themselves. The last of the sunlight leaves the top of Monadnock, and four miles away Main-street lights her electric lamps. It is band night in Main-street, and the folks from Putney, from Marlboro, from Guilford, and even New Fane will drive in their well-filled wagons to hear music and look at the Ex-President. Over the shoulder of the meadow two men come up very slowly, their hats off and their arms swinging loosely at their sides. They do not hurry, they have not hurried, and they never will hurry, for they are of the country—bankers of the flesh and blood of the ever bankrupt cities. Their children may yet be pale summer boarders, as the boarders, city-bred weeds, may take over their farms. From the plough to the pavement goes man, but to the plough he returns at last.
>
> "Going to supper?"
>
> "Ye-ess," very slowly across the wash of the uncut grass.
>
> "Say, that corn-crib wants painting."
>
> "Do that when we get around to it."
>
> They go off through the dusk, without farewell or salutation, steadily as their own steers. And there are a few millions of them —unhandy men to cross in their ways, set, silent, indirect in speech, and as impenetrable as that other Eastern farmer who is the bedrock of another land. They do not appear in the city papers, they are not much heard in the streets, and they tell very little in the outsider's estimate of America.
>
> And *they* are American. (8)

Of these bedrock people, warped and eccentric though many of them were, Miss Wilkins wrote in *A Humble Romance* and indeed in most of her later books. Their endurance and what Ellen Glasgow writing of their co-religionists in Virginia called their fortitude are their salient characteristics. In dealing at times with these virtues in excessive manifestations—with diseases of the will—Miss Wilkins in no way underrates the dignity and significance of lives led without surrender, or thought of it, under incredible stress and adversity. Like Robert Frost, whose vision of New England character William Dean Howells as early as 1915 compared to hers in his "Easy Chair," Mary Wilkins never permits the merely sordid, the "realistic," to becloud the entire picture.

II *The Possibility of "Beauty and Grace"*

In *A Humble Romance*, the title story of the volume presents two lonely, obscure people who manage to generate beauty and happiness in their commonplace lives. Sally, an orphan brought up as a servant girl by an exacting and mean-tempered village woman, suddenly belies her reputation for mousy timorousness by walking out of her mistress' kitchen and marrying a tinker who had happened by in the course of his rounds. The potentiality of revolt in meek and downtrodden natures is a favorite theme with Miss Wilkins; she relates it to a theme of the unpredictability and limitless capacities of the human will. Sally makes her choice in a matter of minutes, while her mistress is in the attic hunting up old rags with which to pay the tinker. More important, Miss Wilkins makes this sudden revolt plausible. She does so by presenting it not only as a revolt but as a conversion from submission to self-fulfillment. The change is entirely within Sally, and it takes place with no enhanced feelings of rancor, which she has never felt towards her employer. She simply decides to leave one sort of life for another. Heroics play no part in the process. "Whether it was by the grace of God, or an inheritance from some far-off Puritan ancestor, the fire in whose veins had not burned low, she could see, if she saw nothing else, the distinction between right and wrong with awful plainness. Nobody had ever called her anything but a *good* girl. It was said with a disparagement, maybe, but it was always 'a good girl.' . . . She looked at her lover and began to believe in him, and as soon as she began to believe in him—poor, unattractive, ignorant little thing that she was!—she began to love just like other girls" (6-7). Many of Miss Wilkins' browbeaten people explode into violent revolt, malicious and destructive. But there is nothing violent about Sally's change, and perhaps that is why it is so final.

Thus, surprisingly to herself as much as to others, Sally proves capable of making and acting upon a momentous choice. Other potentialities now emerge. Her honest tinker husband, who loves Sally and to whom she is devoted, discovers that his first wife, who long ago had left him and whom he thought was dead, is actually alive. When the man she had run off with in turn deserted her, she sought out her husband and demanded his support on pain of his being exposed as a bigamist. The tinker departs, leaving Sally a letter promising that he will return if he is ever able to and urging her to "bear up." He does not explain why or to what destination he is leaving. But Sally's faith in the husband who has led her into a new and better life is more than sufficient for mere "bearing up." Endurance and patience are part of her spiritual heritage, as is initiative. She draws heavily on these legacies. During the years her husband is away, the captive of his former unhappiness, she takes over his peddling, driving his wagon about the countryside. When he is finally released by the death of his wife, he returns and the two remarry with unimpaired love and undiminished gratefulness to life.

The story, especially in summary, may seem sentimental; but—what matters more—it may also be true to life. In both Randolph and Brattleboro Miss Wilkins had known girls who, like Sally, endured the interminable bleakness of a kitchen-maid's dollar-a-week servitude, and she had been well acquainted with the peddlers who in those days roamed the New England countryside. The question implicit in this and many of her stories is: are such lives doomed to perpetual dreariness and insignificance, or can they be redeemed by qualities latent in the victims themselves? Miss Wilkins finds that "beauty and grace" (16) are possible even in such lives and are attainable in terms of values and forces inherent in the New England cultural background.

The possibility of "beauty and grace" is always present, but it does not always materialize. Too often a life is allowed to slip by without realization of its potential, and the Jamesian tragedy of the unfulfilled existence occurs. In their dealing with human motivations Henry James and Miss Wilkins have, in fact, much in common. James attributed the failure to achieve fulfillment both to a headstrong independence of will, as with Daisy Miller or Isabel Archer, and to feebleness of will, as in the case of Daisy's American lover Winterbourne or Isabel's cousin Ralph. And in James's work, as in Miss Wilkins', the men more often than not are weaker-willed than their women. It is not surprising to learn that James followed Miss Wilkins' books with interest.

III *Aboulia*

If Sally's chief asset is an unswerving determination, others of Miss Wilkins' characters are weak-willed to the point of aboulia. Such is Caroline Munson in "A Symphony in Lavender." She has lost her chance for happiness because she cannot make up her mind as to the meaning of a dream. When the story opens, she is an elderly and genteel spinster, living alone with an old servant in the ancestral mansion where she keeps up her pretensions as a charming hostess. From her own lips the reader learns that in her youth she had dreamed that she met a young man to whom she was first attracted but for whom her feelings soon changed to disgust. Later, in real life, she meets a man, an artist, who resembles the man in the dream. She finds him charming and even comes to love him, but clouding her love is a consciousness of latent "horror of him" (46). When he proposes to her, the horror wells to the surface; he has become revolting to her and she regards him as evil. Of course, she rejects him. But for the rest of her life she speculates as to whether her dream was an omen from God or a "nervous whim." She can only hope it was the former, for then in rejecting her lover she would have been acquiescing in divine will—ample justification, in the mind of a daughter of the Puritans, for any act, however unreasonable. But to Miss Wilkins, as to the reader, Caroline Munson's timidity—her failure to force herself to see the truth that she was afraid of marriage—has little to do with God. It stems from her own emotional immaturity, a stunting of the will. To live with her lilacs and her Bible and her constant prayers was easier than to live with a husband. So decreed her unconscious will, the only will she had.

IV *The Pride of the Poor*

Caroline's case is common in Miss Wilkins' writings. With some variations, it is comparable to that of Louisa Ellis, the heroine of "A New England Nun." But more frequently an excess, rather than a deficiency of will, blights the lives of Miss Wilkins' women in *A Humble Romance* and also impoverishes the spirit. In "A Taste of Honey" a young girl, Inez, sets out to pay off cent by cent the mortgage on the family farm that her father, now dead, had striven a lifetime to free of debt. She refuses to marry until she has accomplished this purpose, though she has an eager lover. On the day she makes her final payment, this lover, weary of delay, marries another girl. Inez puts on a brave face and treats her mother and herself to a taste of the honey which hitherto they had always sold to help raise the mortgage money. The mother says to her daughter: "But I should think losin' your beau would take all the sweetness out of the honey." And Inez answers: "I guess there's a good many folks find it the same way with their honey in this world" (106).

It is not the loss of her beau that has taken the sweetness out of Inez's honey, but her realization of the wrongness of immolating herself for a mortgage. But "the pitiful spectacle of her poor, dull father working all his life for such a small aim in such small ways, in vain, haunted her" (103). Pride for herself and for her dead, defeated father forced her to carry on where he left off, even at the cost of the fulfillment of her own womanhood. In this early volume Miss Wilkins was already engrossed by the miseries of rural poverty and its psychological effects on its victims. Later she devoted whole novels to the subject, exploring more deeply the relationship between poverty and pride. At this stage, however, her probings did not go beyond the proverbial concept that the very poor are very proud—and with a pride that sometimes, as with Inez, demands the sacrifice of happiness itself.

Another study of poverty is found in "Old Lady Pingree," an octogenarian of gentle birth who is permitted to take in boarders in her ancestral mansion, though the bank has long since taken it over. She will accept charity but will not acknowledge it. Any gifts, say, of food, must be left surreptitiously behind a door for her to pick up when no one, not even the donor, is looking. Her one accomplishment, the one prop of her precariously tottering pride, is the eighty dollars that she has saved to pay for her burial; for to be buried at the town's expense is the ultimate humiliation, comparable only to ending one's days at the poor farm. Unfortunately, one of Old Lady Pingree's boarders dies before she does, leaving no funds for his funeral. Mrs. Pingree, acting as the village would expect of one of her breeding, promptly lends her own burial sum to the dead boarder's daughter; to do otherwise would utterly demolish her self-respect. Later when the bank sells part of her land to a railway company, she is inveigled into accepting two hundred dollars against her own burial, not as a gift, as the bankers carefully point out (though it is a gift), but as rightfully hers because of an increase in the value of her land. Miss Pingree is entirely satisfied with this arrangement. Not only does it insure her own respectable burial, but it permits her to relinquish claim to the eighty dollars she had loaned to the boarder's daughter.

Indeed, cajoling paupers into accepting any help is one of the problems in village life as Miss Wilkins depicts it. Always the recipient must be made to feel that he is not a receiver of alms; the act of giving becomes an elaborate ritual in which the donor pretends that the needy are doing him a favor by accepting his gifts. Thus in the story "A Mistaken Charity," two destitute old ladies, living entirely on the kindness of their neighbors, are insultingly critical of everything they receive. Were they grateful, they fear, folks might consider them poor enough to be sent to the paupers' home.

V *The Ties of Place*

The villager's attachment to his home, no matter how drab, is the theme of several stories in *A Humble Romance*. In "Brakes and White Vi'lets" Marm Lawson lives with her granddaughter Levina in a house so damp and musty, because of its situation on wet ground, that the child becomes ill and has to be taken away to her father's house in a distant town. So strong are the bonds that attach the old lady to her own house and to the brakes and violets in its dooryard that she would rather live alone than with her son and granddaughter. Once she sets out to visit them but gets no farther than the railroad station in the next village. When the train comes, she does not board it but spends the night in the station, returning the next day by the morning coach to her home. Only on her deathbed does she see her son and Levina again. Human ties, though strong, are weaker with her than those of place. Marm Lawson's well-being, if not her sense of values, has been conditioned by the monotony of life in a mildewy house in a village ten miles from the tracks. She is no longer able to sacrifice dull habit for the love of a child. Dehumanization with her is far advanced.

VI *Overrefined Consciences*

In other stories in *A Humble Romance* sensitivity exaggerated to the point of morbidity exerts a similarly stunting effect. Sometimes the sensitivity arises from motives in themselves unexceptionable. Such is the case with Adoniram Dill in "In Butterfly Time." Forty years before the opening of the story, Adoniram had been on the point of marrying Rebecca Wheat. But one day, when the hilarity of his spirits got the better of him, he chased a butterfly in the Wheats' garden. Mrs. Wheat made a disparaging remark. Adoniram, who had just experienced conversion and was striving to behave like a Christian, mistakenly assumed that Mrs. Wheat's remarks indicated that she did not like him and thus would prefer not to have her daughter united with him. Rather than force a girl against her mother's wishes, he did what he thought was the Christian thing and broke his engagement. Forty years of celibacy for him and Rebecca ensued. The waste of these years in terms of happiness and personal fulfillment is not diminished when at the age of sixty the misunderstanding is finally cleared up and the two get married.

Adoniram was the victim of an overrefined conscience. So also is Martha Patch in "An Honest Soul." Martha, one of the scores of lonely, impoverished seamstresses who inhabit Miss Wilkins' pages, one day receives orders for patchwork quilts from two customers who leave bundles of rags for her to work with. When she has completed the two quilts, for each of which she will receive one dollar, she discovers that in one of them she has used a small piece of cloth belonging to another customer. She tears the quilts apart and resews them, only to find that she has again made a similar error, which she again unhesitatingly rectifies by redoing both quilts. By this time, having earned no money, she has not eaten for several days. When she finally completes the quilts and is about to deliver them, she faints and lies unconscious on her floor until a neighbor rescues her. Miss Wilkins speculates: "It is a hard question to decide, whether there were any real merit in such finally strained honesty, or whether it were really a case of morbid conscientiousness. Perhaps the old woman, inheriting very likely her father's scruples, had them so intensified by age and childlessness that they had become a little off the bias of reason" (86). Like the romancers of the Middle Ages who would pose to their listeners some question of conduct to be answered with reference to the code of courtly love, Miss Wilkins, half-humorously perhaps, leaves the reader with a question of conscience to be resolved in terms of the religion of John Calvin as modified by three hundred years of transplantation in New England.

VII *Setness of Will*

A sheer fixation of will—whether right or wrong in its direction—is another crippling trait among the people in *A Humble Romance*. "On the Walpole Road" is the story of a man and woman afflicted with this defect. The woman, because of family pressure, marries the man despite her love for another. The man knows her feelings but is determined to marry her. During the wedding ceremony when the parson asks the usual question as to whether there is any impediment to the marriage, the woman says that there is: she loves a man other than her intended husband. But she is so set in her will that once she has decided to marry she proposes to go through with it. Thus two immovable wills are joined in a union which endures until the husband's death brings release more than five years later.

A pettier stubbornness—or cussedness, as the country people called it—is that of the husband in "Gentian," who hates all doctors and medicines. While he is suffering from a prolonged and debilitating illness, his wife gives him doses of gentian in his food unbeknownst to him, and as a result he regains his health. The wife, who is as conscientious as Martha Patch or Adoniram Dill, foolishly tells him of her subterfuge. Next morning the wife cooks a good breakfast, but the husband has already been to the store and bought some food which he proceeds to cook and eat, announcing, "I'm jest a-goin' to make sure I hev some tea, an' somethin' to eat without any gentian in it" (259). As he refuses to let his wife cook any of his meals in the future, she asks whether he would not prefer to have her go to her sister's to live. He agrees that "mebbe 'twould be jest as well" (260), and so the two live apart until a return of the husband's illness breaks his stubbornness and he begs his wife to come back and doctor him.

VIII *Revolt*

Sometimes the energies of the will are directed into rebellion rather than into persistence about some whimsical course. In "A Tardy Thanksgiving," Mrs. Muzzy, a widow, decides that she has nothing to be thankful for and hence will spend Thanksgiving Day doing her pig work: preparing and packing the pork she has recently had slaughtered. For a New England woman to ignore such an important religious observance amounts to open revolt against family, neighbors, and God. She nevertheless persists, and her niece, Lizzie, who has just been jilted by her beau, wishes to join her. But Mrs. Muzzy objects: "She had an inner consciousness, ever present to herself, that her state of mind was highly culpable, but she undertook the responsibility for herself with sullen defiance. It was another thing, however, to be responsible for a similar state in another" (55). The problem is resolved when Lizzie's beau returns and Lizzie goes off with him much too readily to suit her aunt's sense of propriety. Thus Mrs. Muzzy sets about her Thanksgiving pig work alone. Her rebellion is soon put down, however, when she spills boiling water on her foot. The accident, she decides, has been a punishment from God; and having received this recognition from the Deity, she is content to sit down to her turkey and plum pudding.

Another story of rebellion is "A Moral Exigency," in which a minister's daughter, who hates life in a parsonage, refuses to marry a widower clergyman with four children, even though her refusal is extremely embarrassing to her father. Instead, she sets her cap at another girl's wealthy suitor and manages to win him for herself. Only when her rival is at the point of death from heartbreak does she relent, undergoing what resembles a conversion. Her "strong will broke down before the accusations of her . . . conscience, which were so potent as to take upon themselves material shapes" (232). But she has had her day of revolt and, most important, has escaped from her father's colleague.

IX *Special "Faculties"*

Most notable among all these headstrong villagers is that they act in accordance with their own wish, whim, or compulsion, usually to their own detriment. But not always. At least two stories in *A Humble Romance* deal with characters who possess definite talents which they somehow find scope to exercise. In "Souvenirs" Nancy Weeks, a seamstress, has produced what passes in the village as an outstanding work of art. It is a wreath made of the hair of her relatives and ancestors, woven to resemble various flowers. Monstrosity spawned of sickly sentimentality though it is, it represents the apogee of the village woman's creativity and has won her renown among the townspeople.

On a higher level is the mathematical talent of Mrs. Wilson Torry in "An Old Arithmetician." Mrs. Torry so loves to play with numbers that her highest pleasure, as she tells her parson, would be "to count up all the beautiful things in this creation. Just think of countin' all them red an' gold-colored leaves, an' all the grapes an' apples in the fall; an' when it comes to the winter, all the flakes of snow, an' the sparkles of frost . . ." (370). So adept is she at "sums" that the minister and the local schoolmaster bring her problems that they themselves cannot solve. She is proud of her "faculty," which she considers to be her one distinguishing mark; for she believes that every one, no matter how poor or uneducated, has been given some particular ability or gift that sets him apart from all others.

One day the minister brings Mrs. Torry an exceptionally recalcitrant "sum." She sets to work on it enthusiastically, applying herself with no awareness of the passage of time. Hours slip by. Her granddaughter returns from school but finds no lunch ready. She returns to school and comes home again in the late afternoon. The grandmother is still puzzling over the sum, fearful now that she has lost her faculty. The girl asks permission to accompany another girl on a train trip to a nearby town. Only half-hearing the request, the grandmother grants it and continues her labors. Late in the evening she is interrupted by the schoolmaster who brings the news that the granddaughter did not return on the train with the other girl. A search is immediately undertaken, while Mrs. Torry is racked by pangs of remorse for forgetting even to feed the child and for giving a permission that she should never have granted. Bitterly, she says she is happy she has been unable to solve the mathematical problem. It is a just punishment that she is losing her faculty. But on the fourth day after the girl's disappearance she is tempted again. "O Lord! I wonder if I was to blame? 'Twas the way I was made, an' I couldn't help that. P'rhaps I should hev let Lettie gone, an' she'd been lost, anyway. I wonder if I hev lost my faculty?" (379). Her rationalization is in terms of the local theology. The Lord made her as she is. It has been predestined that she do sums. So she plunges back into her work, only to be aroused when Letty is brought home unharmed, which happens just as she has solved the problem.

X *"I ain't going to give it up yet"*

Pride, whim, stubbornness, habit, sensitivity, indecision, rebelliousness, monomania plague Miss Wilkins' characters. Sometimes these frailties come into conflict with like ones in other people, sometimes with the consciences of the sufferers themselves, sometimes with both. Resulting from such conflicts, a change of heart, a quasi-conversion, may occur as in the case of the husband in "Gentian" or of the widow in "A Tardy Thanksgiving." Or there may be no change, as in "On the Walpole Road," "An Honest Soul," or "Old Lady Pingree"; stubbornness, pride, or "setness" prevails unabated. The most remarkable example of the latter in *A Humble Romance* is "A Patient Waiter," in which the main character, the old maid Fidelia Almy, refuses to admit that she has been jilted by her lover who left her forty years ago to seek in California the money that would enable them to get married but has not written her a single line since the day of his departure. Twice every day during all that time she has tramped the mile to the post office and back, even on Sundays when there is no mail, to pick up the letter that never comes. At home, she has refreshments ready for her momentarily expected lover. With her lives her niece, Lily Almy, who for a long time shares Fidelia's dream and believes in it. Later, when Fidelia is in her last illness, Lilly herself makes the daily trips to the post office, though by now she knows her aunt is insane and has been all her life. There is nothing to do but to humor her as with her last breath she exhorts her niece to hurry for the mail: "He—promised he'd write, an' . . . *I ain't goin' to give it up yet*" (414).

XI *Confession and Repentance*

The most satisfying stories are those in which a change of heart does occur, and among these the most impressive is "A Conquest of Humility." Lawrence Thayer fails to appear for his wedding with Delia Caldwell. All the couple's relatives—and these constitute most of the population of the village—have gathered at the bride's home. After a long wait Lawrence's father arrives to announce shamefacedly that his son refuses to come. The assumption is that he has fallen in love with pretty Olive Briggs, a salesgirl in a local store, and intends to marry her. Delia meets the situation by a brutal suppression of her feelings, her chief motivation being not to give way to her humiliation before the townspeople. She forces herself to walk among the guests and offers to return their gifts. She gets a schoolteaching job and resumes her former life. When she meets Lawrence, for whom she harbors a strong and angry contempt, she passes him without a look. At church she stares boldly at him and Olive. But there comes a day when Olive jilts Lawrence and Delia has her revenge. " 'I wonder how *he* feels,' " she says to herself. "She saw Lawrence Thayer, in her stead, in the midst of all that covert ridicule and obloquy, that galling sympathy, that agony of jealousy and betrayed trust. They distorted his face like flames; she saw him writhe through their liquid wavering" (429).

Lawrence is in fact jeered at by his mates, but "he went about doggedly. He was strong in silence . . ." (429). Delia and Lawrence could easily have perpetuated their stubborn, silent hate through the remainder of their lives—as so often happens in Miss Wilkins' stories. Their humiliation and resentment could be buried under taciturnity, which would harden their spirits to granite. The only hope for a renewal of their lives is for at least one of them to make a step from humiliation with its exaggerated pride and bitterness to humility with its restoration of spiritual tranquillity. This is the Christian way; it is also the Calvinistic way. First must come confession of the wrongness of one's hate; next, repentance. In the Puritan tradition, from the earliest records of the Massachusetts Bay Colony, a malefactor was expected to confess his sin and voice his repentance before the congregation of his church. Hawthorne, greatly admired by Miss Wilkins, was fascinated by the spiritual implications of public confession and made it the sole basis upon which the erring Arthur Dimmesdale in *The Scarlet Letter* could achieve peace of mind. Similarly, Dostoyevsky, whom Miss Wilkins had also read and admired, stressed public confession as an indispensable and final step in the transformation of pride into Christian humility.

Miss Wilkins may have been writing directly from her knowledge of Puritan psychology and practice, which perpetuated the act of public confession well into the nineteenth century. Or she may have been influenced either by Hawthorne or Dostoyevsky, though this seems less likely. At any rate, the deadlock between Delia and Lawrence, who retain a deeply submerged but substantial remnant of their original love for each other, is resolved by Lawrence's total subduing of his pride. On the second anniversary of the day on which he jilted Delia he asks the former wedding guests to assemble at her house. He admits his guilt, begs Delia's forgiveness, and asks her to marry him. Her answer is: "I never will." Her "whole nature had been set to these words; they had to be spoken" (435). Yet she understands the sincerity of his offer. He is genuinely repentant; he had not rigged this scene as a clever device to win her back now that he had lost Olive. "'A coward and mean.' Yes, he had been, but—Yes, there was some excuse for him—there was. Is not every fault wedded to its own excuse, that pity may be born into the world?" (435-36).

Lawrence is not surprised by the refusal. He knows her "enduring will, her power of indignation" (436). He turns to leave. "There was a certain dignity about him. He had in reality pulled himself up to the level of his own noble, avowed sentiments" (436). Delia gazes after him relentlessly. A girl begins to cry. Delia glances at one of Lawrence's relatives. What she sees makes her spring forward. "You needn't look at him in that way," she cries out. "I'm going to marry him. Lawrence, come back" (436).

What had Delia seen in the woman's eyes that made her so suddenly reverse herself? A moment before Delia had observed, as if in a triumphant dream, all the Thayers and the Caldwells sitting there; and she had thought how they would talk and laugh at Lawrence for his failure. In Mrs. Erastus Thayer's glance Delia had detected the beginning of that ridicule, which would be a perpetual crucifixion for its victim.

XII *"What will folks say?"*

Fully to understand this and many other of Miss Wilkins' stories, one must review the conditions of village life in New England. In some ways there had been little change since colonial times. Miss Wilkins' villages are isolated, somewhat self-sustaining communities, swallowed up in a vast geography much as were the seventeenth-century settlements. Every one knows everyone else; one can be sure one's every action will be scrutinized and commented on according to the code of behavior propagated by the local Congregational Church. One is born into a family whose annual income has been continuously assessed by the villagers with a view to classifying it as poor—a matter of shame—or well-to-do—a matter of satisfaction. On Sabbaths the child attends church perhaps as many as three times; any conspicuous laxness in attendance on the part of his parents arouses strong public disapprobation. Constantly his parents refer their actions to the single standard: "What will people say?" If a child enters the general store and his entrance brings a hush upon the bystanders, he knows at once that his family has been talked about and has had adverse judgment passed upon it. But in any event his clothes will be peered at for signs of poverty; his face for signs of illness. And the findings, whatever they are, will contribute towards the villagers' estimate of his family's material and spiritual status. The child's own conduct, too, will be examined and judged. Does he study hard? Does he help his father and mother willingly with their chores? Does he refrain from profanity and other bad habits? Is he courteous, neat, respectful of his elders?

When the boy or girl reaches adulthood, attraction to the opposite sex begins. Two young people walk home from church together several mornings. A boy calls a few times at a girl's house on Sunday evenings, and the two sit in the mildew-smelling parlor. Such is the courtship in nineteenth-century New England. The rest of the town will, of course, have closely observed these proceedings, and after a few repetitions it will pronounce the couple engaged. Marriage may take place immediately or at any time within the next ten, twenty, or thirty years. If the relationship is broken off, the one responsible for the break will be subjected to condemnation and the jilted to ridicule. Many have wondered why the practice of bundling was permitted in colonial

New England. The answer is simple. By the time a couple reached the bundling stage they would be as good as married in the eyes of the town, and those eyes constituted stronger bonds than any civil or religious ceremony.

After marriage, of course, the couple will be kept under the closest watch, not so much for the detection of any marital infidelity, so unthinkable as to be almost ruled out as a possibility, but for any deviation from the norm, especially in fulfillment of religious and family duties. And, of course, the couple will be among the scrutinizers as well as among the scrutinized; for everyone is everyone else's keeper. Any misconduct, any eccentricity, is a matter of public concern. The confession of one's sin before a church congregation and a request to the membership for forgiveness are merely extensions of the conditions of everyday village life.

What Delia sees, then, in the eyes of the village gossip, Mrs. Erastus Thayer, is a glimmering of the hell of public mockery and revilement that awaits Lawrence once he passes through her doors jilted and a jilter. Her vision moves her pity, and her sense of justice is repelled by the disproportionate fury and duration of Lawrence's punishment at the hands of the townspeople. Knowing from personal experience the agony he will suffer, she does the one thing that will save him; she accepts his offer of marriage. His bloodthirsty tormentors are at once appeased. He has done what is right, and it has brought results. But, more significant for him and Delia, they have both progressed from the pride engendered by their humiliation, to humility—the only pathway to a life of peace and love.

XIII *"An Old House and an Old Woman"*

According to Willa Cather, Sarah Orne Jewett once made the remark that when "an old house and an old woman came together in her brain with a click, she knew a story was under way."[1] Apparently Miss Wilkins' brain clicked in the same manner. Hers is a woman's world, especially in the earlier stories. As one critic facetiously puts it, "In the census of a Mary Wilkins Freeman village the proportions of inhabitants would approximate sixty women upwards of seventy years old, five old men, fifteen middle-aged women, eight middle-aged men, seven girls, three eligible bachelors, two children."[2] The setting for most of her stories, if they should be dramatized, would be very simple; nine tenths of the action takes place in a kitchen, the other tenth in the best parlor. Out-of-doors nature is seen and appreciated, but from the kitchen window or during a walk to the village store to replenish the kitchen supplies. The grander aspects of nature—mountains, lakes, the ocean—are almost entirely lacking.

Among the New England peasantry—and as one reads Miss Wilkins' work one realizes there is such a peasantry, with most of the virtues and vices of the species—the women do not work in the fields and the stables, both of which are the exclusive domain of the menfolk. The division of the spheres of activity is very sharp. On a New England farm of just a generation ago, a farmer's wife might go for years without even entering the barn. The farmhouse is the woman's realm and one which Miss Wilkins knew well because of her intimacy with the Wales family in Randolph. Cooking, sewing, the amassing of trousseaux, the care of house pets (especially cats) and, occasionally, children, and the cultivation of flowers are the activities that occupy the farm or village woman. Thus Miss Wilkins' stories are rich in the description of interiors as accurate and vivid as those in Mark Twain's books. The kitchen with its hearth or stove; the best parlor, smelling of unheated gentility, with its knickknacks, Bible, albums and horsehair sofa; the bare wooden furnishings of the bedchambers; the dooryard with its hollyhocks and shade trees—these she presents with a loving care and an accuracy that give her stories standing as documents in social history.

If Miss Wilkins' world is a woman's world, it is also a world largely of single women—another reflection of real-life conditions. The Civil War and the westward migrations had decreased the number of men. Miss Wilkins' young women and girls have one main goal in life: to find a husband in a scarce market. So intense is their purpose that when it is thwarted the resultant stresses are the stuff of drama. Nor do the women submit easily to defeat; the case of Fidelia Almy, who nursed her hope for forty years, is not untypical of a Mary Wilkins story.

An old woman in an old house is, indeed, for Miss Wilkins as for Sarah Orne Jewett, a perfectly typical situation. But in the Wilkins story, unlike the Jewett one, the old woman will be undergoing some sort of spiritual crisis—a rebellion, a wrestling with her conscience, an unprecedented exertion of the will. Sometimes in the case of a very old maid a marriage takes place, but the story has essentially dealt with her spinsterhood. A story that might be called archetypal in *A Humble Romance* and in Miss Wilkins' later work is "An Object of Love," which Sarah Orne Jewett, incidentally, found to be a model of short fiction. The elderly maiden Ann Millett lives alone with her cat in a tiny, white-painted house with a door and one window in front and a little piazza, "over which the roof jutted, and on which the kitchen door opened, on the rear corner" (266). As the story begins, Miss Millet is taking in her squash because of the possibility of a frost. She is resigned, on the surface, to her lot: "I'd orter be thankful. I've got my Bible an' Willy [the cat], an' a roof over my head, an' enough to eat an' wear; an' a good many folks hev to be alone, as fur as other folks is concerned, on this airth. An' p'rhaps some other woman ain't lonesome because I am, an' maybe she'd be one of the kind that didn't like cats, an' wouldn't hev got along half as well as me. No: I've got a good many mercies to be thankful for—more'n I deserve. I never orter complain" (268).

So Miss Millet has made herself a life keeping house for her cat, attending church with unbroken regularity, and assuring herself twenty times a day that she "orter be thankful." But, were she really thankful, she would not have to remind herself so often. Revolt against God's predestined plan for her life is latent within her. And revolt erupts one night when she returns from prayer meeting to find that Willy has disappeared and is not to be found after a search of several days. In "A Tardy Thanksgiving," a widow refuses to thank the God who has taken her husband from her; and Miss Millet, in full rebellion for the first time in her life, refuses to attend a meeting to worship a God who has deprived her of all companionship except that of a cat and now has taken even it: "Ann Millet, in spite of all excuses that could be made for her, was for the time a wicked, rebellious old woman. And she was as truly so as if this petty occasion for it had been a graver one in other people's estimation" (276).

The minister, dull country parson that he is, expostulates heavy-handedly with her. Neighbor children offer other cats. But Miss Millet is iron-willed. She has "a nature which could rally an enormous amount of strength for persistency" (277). When she finally returns to a meeting, the parson rejoices. "The cat has come back" says Ann. The cat, indeed, had been locked in her cellar where it had been meowing, unheard by the somewhat deaf Miss Millet, until a neighbor had detected its presence. Ann had let the cat into the cellar before going to prayer meeting and on returning had forgotten she had done so.

Had she unconsciously resented the cat which had been a substitute in her life for husband and children? Miss Wilkins doesn't answer the question—or ask it, for that matter. But beyond doubt she expects the reader to ask it for himself and to answer it affirmatively. Miss Wilkins had a personal knowledge about single ladies and their cats. When she was left without parents or sister to live alone in Brattleboro and Randolph, she, too, cherished a cat and experienced distress when it disappeared. She was deeply interested in the relationships between human beings and animals, relationships by no means solely of affection free of resentment or other destructive emotions.

XIV *"Like the best modern work everywhere"*

Any reader of Miss Wilkins' story collections soon becomes aware that she combines in her fiction humor with tragedy and pathos. In summaries of the stories, the humor may not be apparent, and in certain stories it undoubtedly is non-existent. But Martha Patch's sewing and resewing her quilts in order to get one rag in the rightful place, the two old paupers superciliously criticizing the gifts that keep them alive, Adoniram Dill feeling he is unwanted because he is censured for chasing a butterfly, Fidelia Almy visiting the post office twice a day for forty years, though she has received not a single letter in all that time—those foibles elicit laughter as well as tears.

Miss Wilkins sometimes injects humor into an otherwise serious situation by the device of understatement, which in turn is a characteristic of New England speech. When Lucy Tollet, the wife in "Gentian," suggests that she might as well leave her husband since he won't let her cook for him any more, he laconically answers, "Mebbe 'twould be jest as well." The calmness of the phrasing is so inappropriate to the gravity of the step being taken —the breakup of a marriage of half a lifetime—that the reader cannot restrain a smile. Yet a passionate tirade on the part of either the wife or the husband would have been disastrous to the story. The tone of what Alfred Tollet says is just right, not only because it is exactly what he would have said as a New England countryman, but also because it saves by irony what otherwise would have been mere melodrama. Unconscious irony on the part of the character involved also lends humor to "In Butterfly Time." Adoniram, having broken his engagement forty years ago because of his fiancée's mother's slighting remarks, finally learns that no offense had been intended. Adoniram's mother then asks if he is going over to see his sweetheart and make it up with her. "I guess not tonight, mother." "Well, mebbe *'tis* jest as well to wait till tomorrer. I don't want Mis' Wheat to think you was in too much of a rush" (326).

Everywhere Miss Wilkins shows herself adept at capturing the understatement, the irony, the cautiousness of New England rural speech. She is also skillful in preserving the rhythms of this speech, a fact that becomes painfully evident when, in later books, she has Virginians and others speaking in a Yankee cadence. But in her New England stories the effect is most felicitous, and she makes liberal use of dialogue to carry as much of her action as possible. Nor does she make the mistake of so many local-color writers who attempt a phonetic transcription of dialect. Miss Wilkins uses misspellings charily, just enough to indicate the flavor of the language she records. Her Vermonters and her Massachusetts people speak alike, which is linguistically not quite the case, though the two areas are roughly in the same dialect region. She makes no claims like Mark Twain's to the effect that he employed five varieties of Missouri patois in *Huckleberry Finn.* Rhythmically, New England speech tends to be the same throughout the six states; and these rhythms, which she doubtlessly produced without effort from her own speech patterns, provide the distinguishing marks of her dialogue—as well as of much of her narrative and exposition.

In an age when literary style, under the guidance of Howells, Mark Twain, and Sarah Orne Jewett, was abandoning rhetoric and verbosity for directness and simplicity, Miss Wilkins' writing was very modern. Her style anticipates the concreteness and straightforwardness of such writers as Sherwood Anderson, Hemingway, and the Gertrude Stein of *Three Lives.* Image-making words of Anglo-Saxon origin, simple or compound sentences, but few complex ones, and repetition of key words and phrases characterize her early writing. The opening paragraph of "An Old Arithmetician," which is typical, comes directly to the point; it appeals to several of the senses; it is as uncomplicated as a primer; it contains only one figure of speech and that an unobtrusive one. It could, in fact, have been written by Gertrude Stein or Ernest Hemingway: "A strong, soft wind had been blowing the day before, and the trees had dropped nearly all their leaves. There were left only a few brownish-golden ones dangling on the elms, and hardly any at all on the maples. There were many trees on the street, and the fallen leaves were heaped high. Mrs. Wilson Torry's little door-yard was ankle-deep with them. The air was full of their odor, which could affect the spirit like a song, and mingled with it was the scent of grapes" (368).

It has been said that Miss Wilkins wrote thus simply because she was incapable of a more involved style. Later, to be sure, she attempted a more rhetorical manner but with disastrous results. In her early writing she was more likely under the influence, perhaps an unconscious one, of the Bible, which is also concrete in diction and uncomplex in sentence structure. Also she may have been impressed by the naturalness of her fellow New England regionalist, Sarah Orne Jewett. But the direct influence of New England conversational style, itself resonant with Biblical echoings, should not in any event be overlooked. Miss Wilkins' biographer, Edward Foster, surmises that much of her material came from stories told her by country women—dressmakers, relatives, and friends in and around Brattleboro and Randolph. Some of the tales of these gossips would have been told and retold so frequently that they would have acquired an economy of diction and a dramatic quality even in their oral form. Needless to say, they would be lacking in the adornments of "literary writing." One story in *A Humble Romance*, "On the Walpole Road," is in fact told in the form of a gossip session between two old women riding in a buggy along a country highway. They speak first of the threatening weather and then of their horse, and finally they drift into a story of local interest. Most of Miss Wilkins' stories, of course, are without this sort of framework; but their content is of the stuff that gossip thrives on; and, though pruned of most of the digression common to gossip, they are told in the colloquial language of the New England village, with the earthy irony typical of that speech.

Writing in the "Editor's Study" in *Harper's New Monthly* for September, 1887, W. D. Howells gave praise that was typical of the reception accorded Miss Wilkins' work. The stories in *A Humble Romance*, he wrote, "are good through and through, and whoever loves the face of common humanity will find pleasure in them. They are peculiarly American, and they are peculiarly 'narrow' in a certain way, and yet they are like the best modern work everywhere in their directness and simplicity" (640). He compares them to Turgenev's and Björnson's work in their lack of rhetoric. Such writing he considers to be in the air of the period. One author does not copy it from another. Though Howells finds that some of the stories in *A Humble Romance* suffer from sentimentality, this is far from a ruinous defect. As a group, they give a complete representation of New England village and farm life. The best of her work he compares favorably with Sarah Orne Jewett's. Howells, of course, had encountered many of the stories in *A Humble Romance* as they had appeared in the Harper periodicals, and he had already formed an opinion of them. His remarks, in fact, are a justification for his own editorial policy, announced earlier in his inaugural "Easy Chair" essay, in which he had deplored the shallowness and showiness of much of the writing of the day and then had singled out Miss Wilkins, Miss Jewett, and Henry James as notable exceptions to the rule—high praise for an author who at that time had not yet published a volume for adult readers!

CHAPTER 3

A New England Nun

BY 1891 Miss Wilkins had published enough additional stories, mainly in the Harper periodicals to make another collection. *A New England Nun and Other Stories*, as the volume was titled, contains a half dozen or so pieces that rank with her very best, as well as a number of second- or third-rate quality. Its heights of excellence and depths of mediocrity exceed those of *A Humble Romance,* which maintained a consistently high level. *A New England Nun* treats no important themes not represented in the earlier collection, but it emphasizes some, like that of revolt, by more frequent treatment. The settings, too, are likewise suggestive of either Vermont or of eastern Massachusetts or a combination of both; Randolph, where by 1891 she had been living for more than six years, is definitely more prominent as a background.

I *Studies in Passivity*

As a thorough student of the will, Miss Wilkins in *A Humble Romance* had presented cases of total atrophy or passivity of the volition. Such stories were "A Symphony in Lavender" and "A Lover of Flowers," the latter dealing with a young man who contentedly substitutes a love of flowers for the love of woman. The title story of *A New England Nun* records a similar case but with greater literary skill. Louisa Ellis and Joe Dagget have been engaged for fifteen years. Joe has been in Australia most of the time, earning money for his marriage. Louisa has remained in her dreamy New England village—her parents have died in the meanwhile—where she gets into a rut of sewing, of caring for her supposedly vicious dog Caesar, of keeping her house spotlessly clean, and, in short, of speeding the process of becoming an old maid. When Joe returns, the two proceed with their wedding plans, but both soon realize—without confessing it to each other—that they no longer are in love. She is loath to change her spinster's routine, and he has become strongly attracted to Lily Dyer, a pretty and passionate girl working for his mother. In this story everyone is too considerate, too self-sacrificing. Rather than hurt one another's feelings, all three principals scrupulously honor the fifteen-year-old engagement. To preserve its sanctity three lives seem doomed to misery. But one evening, while she is taking a stroll, Louisa overhears Joe and Lily talking on the road. They are speaking of their love. They deplore their treachery to Louisa and decide to desist from it. Lily will go away; Joe will go through with the marriage. The next evening, when Joe comes to call, Louisa, prompted mainly by her reluctance to change her way of life, releases him. Neither of the two mentions Lily, who is actually not much of a factor in Louisa's decision. Joe and Lily, the reader assumes, soon get married. "Louisa, all alone by herself that night, wept a little, she hardly knew why; but the next morning, on waking, she felt like a queen who, after fearing lest her domain be wrested away from her, sees it finally insured in her possession. . . . If Louisa Ellis had sold her birthright she did not know it, the taste of the potage was so delicious, and had been her sole satisfaction for so long. Serenity and placid narrowness had become to her as the birthright itself" (16-17).

The only didactic sentence in the story is the last one just quoted, and it does not constitute a discordance. It was not necessary, however. With its evocation of the torpid, dusty summertime atmosphere of a remote New England village and with its description of Louisa's manner of living symbolized by her canary singing in its cage and with the merging of the environment and all its exacting pettiness with Louisa's character, this is well-nigh a perfect story—one worthy of standing with the best of Chekhov and Katherine Mansfield.

What has happened to Louisa during her prolonged maidenhood is abundantly clear without the one-sentence statement of it that the author, like Hawthorne, feels compelled to make. Like certain of Henry James's characters Louisa has done no less than permit herself to become unfitted for life. What her passivity has done to her is adroitly symbolized not only by the canary but by her chief pastime, that of distilling the essences from rose petals in a little apparatus she owns and storing the oils away in vials for no foreseeable use. What would become of any man she might marry, were she not wise enough to steer clear of marriage altogether, is symbolized in the fate of Caesar, the luckless dog which has spent fourteen years on a chain because in puppyhood he playfully bit the hand of a neighbor. Having earned the reputation of viciousness, Caesar has never known the joy of barking at a woodchuck or of finding and burying a bone. Nothing that belongs to Louisa may have contact with life. Next to Joe's tracking dust onto her immaculate carpets and disarranging the books on the parlor table, his avowal that he is someday going to unchain Caesar strikes the most terror into her heart. And doubtless Caesar's present bondage arouses fears in Joe as to his future condition if he marries this woman.

When Louisa renounces Joe, she condemns herself to prolongment of her nun's life that only death will terminate. But she also redeems herself to a degree. Too weak to break out of her cage, she at least comes to terms with her inadequacies. Not only does her decision, negative act of will though it is, partly interrupt the unrippled flow of years of passivity, but it marks her as the possessor of a sense of moral realism, which Howells (in *The Rise of Silas Lapham*, for instance) repeatedly declared goes hand in hand with literary realism. To force herself to go through with the marriage, knowing as she does that the honorable Joe stands ready, would make three people miserable; it would be a threefold self-immolation, and nothing more, and hence it would constitute an immoral act which could be excused only by the canons of sentimentality. Joe and Lily were prepared to sacrifice themselves and hence to commit an act of sentimentality, or of immorality, according to Howells' views. And most readers of the day, being sentimentalists, would have approved of such sacrifice. But Louisa, realistically assessing the ingredients of her own and the others' happiness, emerges as the strongest of the trio, pitiable though the barrenness of her own existence may be. Louisa has allowed her life to slip into paralysis over a period of fifteen years; for this she is culpable and for this she pays. As things now are, she will be happier, or less miserable, single than married; and Joe and Lily have an excellent chance of a full life together. When Howells referred to Miss Wilkins' realism, as he often did, it was as much to her sense of moral rightness, as opposed to sentimental rightness, as to her accurate depictions of rural life.

Another study of passivity is "A Village Lear," the story of a superannuated cobbler, Barney Swan, whose sole pleasure is to putter about all day in his tiny dooryard shop. Because he feared he might squander his money, he has given it, Lear-like, to his two married daughters, Malvina and Ellen. They feed him, provide him with a bed in his former house, and permit him the use of his beloved shop. Their toleration of him goes no further. When his granddaughter Annie is to be married, Barney sells his watch to buy her a present; but he is not allowed to go to the wedding since he has no suitable clothes and would only be in the way. He tries to give Annie the present as the bridal couple are leaving, but she is whisked away before she can respond to his cries: "Annie! Annie! jest look a-here! See what Gran'pa's got for ye!" (284).

Eventually, Malvina decides to have the shop torn down, for she considers it an eyesore. In despair, Barney flees to the cottage of a young couple who had previously befriended him. His health has been failing ever since the wedding, and he soon dies. Barney has been a victim all his life, first of the shoe factories, which deprived him of his livelihood as a handicraft shoemaker, and then of his daughters, who pushed him out of their lives once they had his money. He is a pitiable rather than a tragic character, accepting without a struggle his fate of being repeatedly discarded. The comparison that the title invites with the protagonist of Shakespeare's tragedy is misleading: Barney and Lear have little in common except ungrateful daughters.

In Miss Wilkins' stories, New England villages were the habitat of termagants whose ferocious wills reduced their luckless menfolk to a state of whimpering subserviency. The totally passive male appears again in the story "A Kitchen Colonel," in which a henpecked husband, a failure all his life, is reduced in his old age to the position of scullery maid in his wife's kitchen. So complete is his bondage that he cannot get an hour off to attend a special town meeting. Long since lacking the backbone to help himself, he is able to help his orphaned granddaughter escape from a like fate. The one time that his wife releases him, for a day trip to Boston with a crony, he discovers that his absence will necessitate the granddaughter's remaining home from a picnic during which there is reason to believe that her beau will "come to an understanding with her." The morning the husband was to go to Boston, he voluntarily calls off the journey, eliciting the jeers of "kitchen colonel" from the friend he was to have accompanied. The granddaughter goes on to the picnic, is proposed to, and is duly married. The wedding is a scene of comedy: the old man, just before the minister pronounces the words that bind the couple, is ordered to the kitchen to rescue some boiling milk and thus does not witness the marriage that he had made possible.

Before leaving the theme of passivity, one must glance at "Sister Liddy," which instead of the humor, sentiment, or pathos that informs the other stories of atrophied will, exudes an atmosphere of utter despair and futility. In mood it is the strongest story Miss Wilkins ever wrote. In the town poorhouse, which also serves as a madhouse, the sane and the insane poor share an unmitigated wretchedness. The time is late autumn, when chilly rains slant across fields of stubble. The house itself is a barracks with long empty corridors and bleak common rooms through which echo the laughter of playing children, the shrieks of the lunatics, the moans of the sick, and the sighs of the paupers. Most notable among the many characters introduced are a tall insane woman who predicts the imminent end of the world; a fat old woman with no brain to be demented, who amuses herself with malicious gossip and spiteful comment about the other inmates; a pretty old woman who finds solace in her long-past reputation as a belle; Polly Moss, a pitiable pauper who has had nothing in her life worth remembering but is kindhearted and amuses herself and the children by playing ball with them; Sally, who spends her days tearing her bed to shreds; a young woman, sick and melancholy and deserted by her lover; and the impassive matron, Mrs. Arms, who presides over this inferno as stolidly as if it were a chicken coop full of placidly clucking hens.

There is no plot to speak of. The inmates wander on and off the stage like the people in Gorky's *Lower Depths*, which in no way surpasses Miss Wilkins' story as a "naturalistic" study of the despair arising from social degeneration. Sometimes one of the insane erupts into violence, but in general the dreary routine goes on uninterrupted.

The title of the story derives from Polly Moss's invention of a beautiful Sister Liddy to combat the boastings of the other women as they recall their past lives. Polly had no past any more than she had a sister, but her stories of her imagined sister put to shame anything the others can conjure up from the drab desolation of their lives. Sister Liddy sang like an angel, dressed like a princess, was married to a fabulously wealthy husband, and lived in Boston. Polly's dimwitted listeners half believe her, perhaps because it is less boring to believe than to disbelieve. But Polly, among her other miseries, suffers from a New England conscience; and two weeks later, while dying of pneumonia, she confesses her deceit to a group assembled at her bedside. With her confession the story closes.

Like "A New England Nun," "Sister Liddy" lacks the happy ending that literary fashion induced Miss Wilkins almost invariably to impose on her stories. To be sure, as Polly is dying, the melancholy, lonesome young woman ecstatically rushes in to announce that her lover has come to take her away. But this unexpected good fortune, if it is that, only intensifies the hopelessness of those who remain. Much better written than Dreiser's stories, "Sister Liddy" puts one in mind of that writer's or Stephen Crane's most naturalistic and deterministic pieces: "Sanctuary," for example, or "An Experiment in Misery." Not that the New England poorhouse deserves a monument, but among all the commemorations of that dreary and inhumane institution "Sister Liddy" stands supreme.

II *Dormant Volcanoes*

If the atrophied will figures importantly in *A New England Nun*, so does its opposite, the overdeveloped will, especially in the process of rebellion against an oppressive environment. Two of Miss Wilkins' very best-known stories, both in this volume, are records of such revolts. The first, and the better written of the two, is "A Village Singer." Candace Whitcomb, the leading soprano in the village choir for forty years, is dismissed because her voice has begun to crack. In her place a younger woman is hired. Candace is informed of her dismissal at a surprise party, at which she is given a photograph album. The next Sabbath, when the new soprano Alma Way sings a solo, Candace shrills out with a different hymn from her house next door to the church. The weather is hot and the windows of both buildings are open, so that the interference is very effective. Mr. Pollard, the minister, calls on the old singer and expostulates with her, but she repulses him with defiance and fury. What enrages Candace is the manner in which she has been let go. "If they'd turned me right out fair an' square, showed me the door, an' said, 'Here, you get out,' but to go an' spill molasses, as it were, all over the threshold, tryin' to make me think it's all nice an' sweet–" (27). Not knowing to whom to return the album, she uses it as a foot rest as she harangues the parson, who "is aghast and bewildered at this outbreak" (28).

Miss Wilkins describes Candace's emotions as "tropical, and more than tropical, for a New England nature has a floodgate, and the power which it releases is an accumulation. Candace Whitcomb had been a quiet woman, so delicately resolute that the quality had been scarcely noticed in her, and her ambition had been unsuspected. Now the resolution and the ambition appeared raging over her whole self. . . . To this obscure woman, kept relentlessly by circumstances in a narrow track, singing in the village choir had been as much as Italy was to Napoleon–and now on her island of exile she was still showing fight" (28-30).

Candace spoils the afternoon meeting as effectively as she did the morning one. Her nephew, who is engaged to Alma Way, tries to reason with her, but she responds by threatening to disinherit him. That evening, before going to bed, she looks out and sees the red glow of a forest fire in the distance. She herself is "in the roar of an intenser fire" (33). She lies awake all night and in the morning she is ill, consumed by the previous day's emotional conflagration. She never rises again. But she has softened enough to apologize to the minister, to assure her nephew that his inheritance is safe, and to ask Alma to sing for her. The ending may be sentimental, but the sentimentality is an expression of the characters rather than of the author. After the single emotional eruption of a lifetime, Candace would inevitably return to the personal and social norm. Even the photograph album, a symbol of extreme sentimentality, would be bearable.

This tale of a volcanic disturbance on the hitherto unruffled surface of an obscure and restricted life reflects one of Miss Wilkins' deepest convictions about New England character. The phenomenon is closely related to the sudden shift in volition that occurs in so many of her stories–a change from mulish antagonism to an acceptance or reconciliation, as in "A Conflict Ended," or simply from an unbending point of view to a more reasonable one, as in "A Tardy Thanksgiving." Miss Wilkins' most widely acclaimed story, at least in her lifetime, "The Revolt of Mother," combines the theme of eruption of passivity into rebellion with that of the suddenly redirected will. Adoniram Penn is as unyielding a New England farmer as any of those who populate Miss Wilkins' pages. For years he has succeeded in dominating his wife Sarah, always postponing the building of a new house he had promised her. But when he builds a new barn instead, he goes too far. While he is away for a week on business, his wife moves herself and her family into the barn and sets up housekeeping there, an act which thrills the village gossips and which shatters her husband's will when he returns. Reduced to tears, Adoniram consents to cut the windows and put up the partitions that will convert the barn into a comfortable dwelling.

In this story there is more humor and less intensity than in "A Village Singer." In fact, its main intention was probably comic. Miss Wilkins in later years was very critical of the story, asserting that in it she sacrificed truth. No woman with the courage or imagination of Sarah Penn, she went on to say, ever existed in New England. A true New England woman of the period would have concurred with her husband in deferring her own comfort to that of the farm animals, on which the family's livelihood depended. Yet Miss Wilkins' own fiction constantly belies this assertion. Her tales abound in strong-minded women capable of withering the most formidable "cussedness" in their menfolk, and by no means all of these women are materialists who would sacrifice the well-being of their families to the greater productivity of the farm. To many of them, flowers or some other object of beauty, some human relationship—above all, their own integrity and sense of worth—may be much more important than money or possessions. While the actual occurrences in "The Revolt of Mother" are outside the realm of probability, the spirit behind them is true to life, especially if allowance is made for the fierce individuality latent in New England village character. The greatest disservice done to this story was President Theodore Roosevelt's comment in a speech that American women would do well to emulate the independence of Sarah Penn. From then on, the story was removed from the category of comic fantasy where it belongs and placed before the public as a serious tract on women's rights, which it surely is not.

III *Self-laceration*

Behind the eccentric stubbornness of some of her characters, Miss Wilkins saw an impulse of self-punishment—self-laceration, as Dostoyevsky called it—arising out of hurt pride—out of humiliation as distinct from humility. The spectacle of human perversity, or irrational, self-destructive action, fascinated her as it did Dostoyevsky and Poe, and in many of her works she probes for the motivation of such irrationality. Thus in "A Poetess," an old maid of fifty who grows flowers rather than the vegetables she needs for her very sustenance, has won a place for herself in the village as a writer of poetry, the sentimentality of which is symbolized by the chirpings of a canary she keeps as her companion in song. One day a bereaved friend asks her to write a poem commemorating her dead baby. The poetess obliges with her mawkish best, and the admiring friend has copies printed and sends them to all her neighbors and relatives. Unfortunately, a copy gets into the hands of the minister, who himself has literary pretensions as well as some discrimination. A gossiping neighbor soon triumphantly reports to the poetess that the parson considers her poem to be trash and the distribution of copies of it to be in extremely bad taste. As she listens, the poetess' face becomes "a pale wedge of ice between her curls" (153). When her gossiping neighbor leaves, she gathers together all her poems, burns them, and deposits the ashes in a tea-pot. But first she vents her feelings to God concerning His dispensation of things: "I'd like to know if you think it's fair. . . . Had I ought to have been born with the wantin' to write poetry if I couldn't write it—had I? Had I ought to have been let to write all my life, an' not know before there wa'n't any use in it? Would it be fair if that canary-bird there, that ain't never done anything but sing, should turn out not to be singin'?" (154-55).

The poetess' notion about her relationship with God and Providence is peculiarly legalistic. It is reminiscent of the old Puritan Federal Theology, according to which God almost literally enters into legally binding covenants with His elect. Thus if one is a full church member by virtue of conversion, or a religious "experience" judged to be valid by the elders, one may assume that he is of the elect with all the immunities and privileges pertaining to that estate and that he comes under the covenant of grace which guarantees salvation through Christ to the chosen. Man and God are under contract to one another.

Now the poetess is a devout church member, and though the Federal, or Covenant, Theology was long since dead, enough of its spirit lingered to make her feel resentful at what seemed a trick played on her by God. "A Tardy Thanksgiving" and "An Object of Love"—which is a story of a maiden lady who will no longer attend meeting after her cat has been lost—record similar resentment at God's seeming failure to live up to His end of the bargain. The intent in all these cases is not only to hurt God, who has humiliated His elect, but to hurt the ego as well. The ultimate motivation in such action is an obscure one, but Dostoyevsky and Gide provide a clue. When humiliated by another, whether God or man, man bolsters his pride and declares his independence by hurting himself. It is a way of asserting in action the words so often spoken by Miss Wilkins' proud-but-poor characters: "I won't be beholden to anybody." The person who insists on hurting himself can logically proclaim that he is responsible to no one but himself. Thus the poetess in the story deprives herself of her sole *raison d'être*, the writing of verse, and dies asserting her selfhood. On her deathbed she requests the minister to bury the ashes of her poems in her grave and to compose a poem in her memory. When he asks why she destroyed her work, she tartly answers: "I found out it wa'n't worth nothin'" (158). But the minister fails to realize that the words should make him feel guilty. He has no idea that he was the cause of her action; and the poor poetess is deprived of even that revenge.

The poetess dies unreconciled, still bitter. In "A Solitary" the recluse Nicholas Gunn achieves a reconciliation with God. Nicholas has lost his beloved wife, and he has suffered other unspecified sorrows and calamities, mainly from folks he "set by." He arrives at a novel solution for getting the better of a cheating life: "I figured out that if I didn't care anything for anybody, I shouldn't have no trouble from 'em; an' if I didn't care anything for myself, I shouldn't have any from myself. . . . I let folks alone . . . an' didn't do anything for myself. I kept cold when I wanted to be warm, an' warm when I wanted to be cold.

I didn't eat anything I liked, an' I left things around that hurt me to see. My wife she made them wax flowers an' them gimcracks [in the room where he is talking]. Then I used to read the Bible, 'cause I used to believe in it an' didn't now, an' it made me feel worse. I did about everything I could to spite myself . . ." (231-32).

Nicholas pursues his masochistic way of life in an unheated cottage on a lonely mountainside. His diet is corn-meal mush and water. On blizzardy days he sits on the steps while the snow piles up on him as if he were one of the boulders in his fields. When a neighbor, sick and exhausted, stops on his way up the mountain to ask for a moment of warmth and shelter, Nicholas surlily permits him to enter the fireless kitchen but does nothing for his comfort. The question is: What can bring Nicholas out of his loathing of himself and reinstate him as a member of the human race from which he has seceded? Whereas in medieval Europe or present-day India he might be popularly venerated as a hermit, saint, or *sannyasin*, in his New England town he is the object of a scorn that only deepens his misanthropy. The way out of his dilemma is perhaps sentimental but one that the sages of most religions, as well as the psychiatrists of our day, agree upon as almost the sole cure of sicknesses like Nicholas's. Love is the sovereign remedy for such ills, and Nicholas benefits from it as much as any one else. Miss Wilkins' formula is precisely that of Dostoyevsky. The self-laceration resulting from the humiliation of the ego terminates only when, through love, one transforms humiliation into humility. The metamorphosis can occur to a Puritan saint or to Dmitri Karamazov. In any human being lies latent the potential of love that can lift him from selfishness into selflessness.

So it is with Nicholas Gunn. Another day the neighbor stops to rest at the hut, and this time he is so ill that even Nicholas permits him to remain and ministers to his comfort. For years Nicholas had used his stove only to cook his mush. Now he lights it to warm his house. With this symbolic act, spiritual thaw sets in. Nicholas invites the ailing old man to live with him. He redirects his energies from self-hurt to helping another. He even begins to feed the sparrows that hop about on the snow outside his house.

IV *The Healthy Will*

In a number of stories in *A New England Nun*, as in *A Humble Romance*, a strong but healthy will is directed toward legitimate ends which it eventually attains after heroic struggle. These are manifestations of the Puritan will at its best; they are proof of its original vigor when it was untouched by decay. "Louisa" is such a story, and it is one of the most skillfully written in the volume. It celebrates the independence of a country girl—a teacher who has lost her job through the nepotism of a school committeeman. She refuses to marry a rich suitor, as her widowed mother desires, but devotes herself to wresting a living from the single acre of land the family owns. Among numerous handicaps she has to overcome is her senile grandfather, who digs up her seed potatoes as fast as she plants them. When not cultivating her own land, she hires herself out as a fieldworker, much to the chagrin of her mother, who is shocked at the idea of a New England girl doing outdoor labor for pay.

Louisa is a finely drawn character, reminiscent of Dorinda Oakley in Ellen Glasgow's *Barren Ground*. Her independence seems as natural as the plants that grow out of the soil she tills; one can admire her refusal to marry her wealthy but arrogant suitor. The story ranks high among Miss Wilkins' stories that deal with pride among the rural poor, and in this case the pride is not pathological but wholesome. Even the happy ending in which the suitor marries the girl who had usurped Louisa's teaching job and thus makes available for Louisa this source of much-needed income is acceptable. The arrangement in no way violates verisimilitude.

"A Church Mouse" deals with the same theme in a lighter manner. Hetty Fifield, having been turned out of the home where she had been living and working for years, decides that she would like to have the job of sexton in the village church. She cajoles the deacon into letting her have the position; against his better judgment, she moves her stove and bed into the meeting-house to live there. The congregation tolerate her for a while, for they couldn't turn her out as they would a cow. "They had their Puritan consciences . . ." (415). But their patience is exhausted when during meeting the mephitic odor of cooking cabbage drifts through the church. The selectmen wait upon the sexton as a group, but fail in their efforts to remove her. The chief selectman goes to get his wife, a woman for whose powers of persuasion he has learned to entertain a high regard; but on returning, he finds that Hetty has barricaded herself into the church as into a blockhouse. Forced to treat with her, the selectmen end by permitting her to remain. On the next day, which is Christmas, Hetty rings the church bells for the first time they have ever been heard in this Puritan town in celebration of the Nativity.

V *Assessment*

In *A Humble Romance* and in *A New England Nun* Mary Wilkins presents a comprehensive and consistent appraisal of New England village life. Contrary to what certain critics and literary historians have said, she does not unconditionally condemn this way of life as narrow and soul killing. Though critical, she does not belong in that literary movement labeled "The Revolt from the Village," which includes such authors as Ed Howe, Hamlin Garland, and Sinclair Lewis. Nor does she wage mortal warfare on vestigial Puritanism. She sees the shortcomings of rural New England character, but she is also aware of its strengths, which also have their roots in Puritanism. As a general thing the people in her fiction are free to work out their destinies by their own devices. Sometimes they become warped, but that is not so damning to the social order as an adherence to a standardized pattern of character would be. Some stories, of course, reveal the evils of gossip and the villagers' intolerance and misunderstanding of any major deviation from the norm, as in the case of the "love-cracked" Christmas Jenny (in the story of that name) whose kindness to animals and birds at the sacrifice of her own proper nutriment prompts what Miss Wilkins calls a witch hunt to set her straight. But in many stories—even in "Christmas Jenny" at the end—the villagers accept eccentricities which entail no serious social harm.

In summary, the following seem to be the major points in Miss Wilkins' evaluation of New England village life:

1. It often is afflicted with poverty, which arouses in her great distress and some indignation against the industrialization and other forces which have brought it about. Country people seldom sit down to a full-course meal except at Thanksgiving. Usually their fare consists of a bowl of soup, or a cup of tea, and bread

or a serving of mush. The poorhouse is a repeatedly presented evidence of the poverty of rural life.

2. Life is often monotonous and lonely, and spinsterhood and celibacy are normal conditions.

3. In these circumstances the people became ingrown, and some of them become bigoted, backbiting, or surly.

4. Many characters assert their independence of the rest of the community and, even though they are branded as "peculiar," succeed in living meaningfully.

5. The townspeople themselves, more often than not, recognize the intrinsic value of this type of struggle, and respect it even when it results in oddness.

6. To offset the loneliness of the lives of so many of the villagers there is among them a solidarity, based on their commonly shared beliefs and widespread participation in church and local government, that gives even the most inveterate solitary the security that arises from a consciousness of "belonging." In such closely knit societies something usually can be arranged to alleviate the distress of all but the most abysmally unfortunate.

Given these conditions, both favorable and unfavorable, the central theme of all of Miss Wilkins' village fiction is the struggle of the individual toward self-fulfillment, whether in marriage, on the farm, in the pulpit, or in the schoolhouse. The environment is a hard one in which to achieve self-realization, and many persons fail; but others are tougher than the environment, and their success speaks well for Yankee tenacity.

The critical reception of *A New England Nun* was generally favorable. Typical were the remarks in an article "New England in the Short Story" in the *Atlantic Monthly* of June, 1891, in which the anonymous reviewer discusses Miss Wilkins' book along with collections by Annie Trumbull Slosson and Sarah Orne Jewett. Among these three he finds Miss Wilkins to be most successful in conveying a feeling for the loneliness of New England rural life and in delineating the remarkably individualized characters—"highly intensified and noticeable persons, though the exaggerations may be of unimportant qualities" (846)—fostered by the religious and political conditions of the region. The writer praises Miss Wilkins' fiction for its lack of sentimentality, its extreme compression, and its reproduction, without resort to phonetic transcription, of the speech of the

New England countryman. For special praise the story "Life Everlastin'" is singled out. It tells of a dreadful dual murder and the consequent conversion of the village agnostic, Louella Norcross, to the Calvinist scheme of salvation when she contemplates the plight of the murderer—a tramp she had once befriended—whose only hope is in the gratuitous grace and forgiveness of God. Though few have followed this reviewer in assigning pre-eminence to "Life Everlastin'," the article did set the tone for most critical evaluation of Miss Wilkins' work.

CHAPTER 4

The Will

EVER SINCE the 1880's Mary Wilkins has been recognized as the anatomist of the latter-day Puritan will. The question of human volition, its freedom from or its dependency on divine decree, had for centuries been a preoccupation of Calvinists both in Europe and America. Miss Wilkins, nurtured in nineteenth-century Congregationalism, which descended directly from the rigid Calvinism of the Reformation, inevitably approached the problem in terms of the theology that was at the very marrow of all her training. To understand her approach, one must examine the religious doctrine in rural New England during her lifetime, especially her earlier years.

I *"Strenuous Goadings of Conscience"*

In Mary Wilkins' day, Calvinistic orthodoxy had softened considerably. Throughout New England the old religion was in conflict with Unitarianism, which had gained control of many of the Congregational churches, especially in the cities. But a Calvinism only slightly modified was far from extinct in most of the villages, and nowhere in New England was its spirit dead. The New England conscience was no less a goad in directing the average life in accordance with the virtues always valued by the Puritans—duty, truthfulness, honesty, thrift. The Nicene Creed held unchallenged sway among those churches that had not gone over to Unitarianism. God was still in his heaven, ready to pass judgment on the deeds of men, smiling or frowning upon their affairs as they merited. Heaven awaited the righteous; hell, the sinner. God's only son, Christ, was the sole means of man's salvation. Full membership as a communicant in a church was still deemed a requisite for eligibility in sharing the benefits of Christ's atonement. Admission to church membership, in turn, depended on the applicant's proof before a board of elders that he had undergone the experience of conversion, that is, an overwhelmingly, emotionally charged surge of conviction of the reality of Christ and a consuming love of Him.

Conversion was, and perhaps still is, the most important episode in the life of any Christian in the sects deriving from Calvinism. Without this all-engrossing sense of assurance that Christ lives in heaven and earth and constitutes the sole access to the future life, any spiritual advance is impossible. At all costs, one must undergo conversion. To aid the spiritually slothful to this end, periods of revival were set aside each year in many New England villages of the last century. Mary Ellen Chase in her autobiographical *A Goodly Heritage* describes the annual revivals in Blue Hill, Maine, the little coastal town in which she grew up. For weeks each winter, while the drive for regeneration progressed, the young people of the town would subject themselves to agonizing soul-searching. After several alternations between ecstasy and despair, a person would usually announce that he found himself in a state of grace–social and family pressures would hardly allow another outcome–and he would be admitted to the Lord's Supper and to full participation in church government. From then on, he could enjoy a well-founded hope for life eternal. Those remaining unaffected, despite the exhortations of preachers, parents, and friends who had already made the grade, sank into a state of self-accusing despair, which later might give way to defiance.

In the colleges, too, the students were annually lashed into similar mass convulsions. In Emily Dickinson's letters, for example, are accounts of the revivals at Mt. Holyoke Female Seminary and of her own consequent agonizings over her inability to yield to them. Never a convert, she may well have owed much of the mental pain of her later life to this youthful worry over her inner state. Any careful reading of the letters discloses that Emily Dickinson never totally rejected the religion of her forefathers. In moments of personal crisis she sought the advice and help of clergymen. Many of her attitudes toward God were strictly Puritan, such as her demands on Him that he live up to certain legalistic standards in his dealings with the human race.

Mary Wilkins also attended Mt. Holyoke Seminary for one year; and in her era the revivals were still being held. One reason for the ill health that caused her to leave was "too strenuous goadings of conscience,"[1] as she later put it. Not only was there a particularly intense revival during her year there—all but ten of the 260 students manifested "interest"—but the rules of the school were such as to overstrain a sensitive conscience. The regimen of daily study, worship, and housework was exhaustingly monotonous. Infractions of the rules were classified according to their severity: among the first-class misdemeanors were absences from church, from recitations, and from meals; ranked as second class were tardiness, untidiness, breaking study hours. Each day a student was required to report all her infractions to one of her teachers. If the teacher thought the lapse sufficiently serious, she would order the girl to sit in the front seat at the Sunday-morning assembly of the entire school, where she would be a public example and do public penance for her misdeeds. This Puritan seminary had some of the atmosphere of a convent, where the nuns are expected to confess their wrongdoings and to be held accountable for them.

New England Puritanism was always in some respects a peculiarly public religion. It has already been noted that the practice from earliest times was to require those who have erred to make public confession. Revivals, of course, are entirely public; and the state of one's soul becomes readily evident by whether or not he proclaims himself converted. Each person's sins and the degree of grace he enjoyed were the concern of the entire community in New England of a hundred years ago. Small wonder that the villages seethed with gossip and that the church itself sanctioned and encouraged speculation as to the inner and outer life of each of its members or would-be members. No wonder that fears of what one's neighbors might think were pivotal in determining one's decisions. Always, it must be emphasized, a person's conduct of his own life was an indication of the state of his soul.

According to orthodox Calvinism one was either among the elect, that is, those destined for salvation, or among those slated for eternal damnation. From the beginning of time one's name was in God's book for one of those destinies. One's personal efforts were to no avail; the doctrine of good works was deemed a heresy. But the elect could expect to undergo conversion and after conversion lead sanctified lives—moral, useful, frugal, righteous ones. Also, they could expect to prosper in their callings, enjoying more material wealth than their unsanctified fellows. On the other hand, failure to experience conversion and lead a prosperous and righteous life indicated that one had been abandoned by God and was bound for everlasting punishment as the just result of Adam's sin perpetuated through all generations.

How desirable it was, therefore, that one's life appear godly and prosperous. No one wished to pass for one of the abandoned of God. Even the converted had to be on their toes, for the genuineness of any conversion could never be entirely certain. Any moral backsliding or loss of money or standing could be construed as an indication that one's conversion was spurious. In the Puritan community there was no infallible rest for either the wicked or the righteous. Constant soul-searching, as exemplified in the diaries of such eminent Puritans as Cotton Mather and Jonathan Edwards, was the norm for the inner life. Constant striving to prove by one's actions and one's material well-being the soundness of one's spiritual condition was the norm for the outer life. Did one's business or farm flourish? Did one become an elder in the church or a selectman in the town government? Did one's family multiply and remain healthy? If the answers to these questions were positive, then one had the satisfaction of assuming that all was well between him and God and of knowing that his fellow townsmen had the same assumption. But if his house burned, his cattle or wife proved barren, or the voters ejected him from office, then he would shiver with mortal apprehension and his neighbors would speculate somberly regarding his chances for salvation.

This state of affairs may be exaggerated in this brief description, but it is reasonably true even for so late a period as the second half of the nineteenth century. To a certain extent it is true also for today, if one places credence in the theories of such writers as Tawney and Weber concerning the "Protestant ethic." In all events, the Calvinist outlook placed a premium on success. It encouraged dogged effort and frantic exertion in reaching a goal that would impress one's neighbors and convince oneself of God's favor.

II *Edwards: "Volitions are necessary events"*

A curious paradox exists in Calvinism, and therefore in a huge segment of Protestantism, regarding the will. Taken at face value, the doctrine of election would seem to nullify the will. If one were not chosen, all the will power in the world would be to no avail. This concept is similar to the one known in the Middle Ages as simple necessity. God foreknows everything; all events must occur as He has foreseen them. Foreknowledge and predestination are synonomous. A believer in simple necessity might logically decide to permit events to roll over him, making no effort to shape his own future, since everything has already been foreordained in the mind of God. In literature an example of this attitude is Chaucer's Troilus, who spends much of his time moaning on his couch, bewailing his harsh fate but doing nothing to balk its inevitable course.

But there is another type of necessity, known as conditional necessity, which postulates that man has freedom of will though God knows what man wills. According to this theory, the will is still a significant agent. Boethius and Milton both embraced this view. In *Paradise Lost* Milton quotes God as saying that Adam and Eve alone ordained "Their own revolt, not I: If I foreknew,/Foreknowledge had no influence on their fault . . ." (Book III). And elsewhere in *Paradise Lost* God asserts: "I made him [man] just and right,/Sufficient to have stood, though free to fall" (Book III).

Milton was, of course, a Puritan writer and *Paradise Lost* is the greatest literary monument to Puritanism. As such, it was as highly venerated in New as in Old England. But, though Milton subscribes to the doctrine of election, he grants somewhat more freedom to man's will than do the most thoroughly orthodox Calvinists. In this he was part of a trend that was to continue unhindered until Jonathan Edwards a century later attempted to narrow once more the limits of human volition. The important point is, though, that many Puritan theorists, certainly including Edwards himself, were deeply preoccupied with the subject of the will and its potentialities. Milton's insistence that man directs his own life by vigorous use of the will is typical.

Whatever theory they adopted concerning the will, most Puritans saw in its exertion both a duty and a virtue. One should struggle unflaggingly to achieve conversion, for example, even though it is a matter of God's predestination. One should strive to be sanctified after conversion, though sanctification, too, depends solely on God's pleasure. As Perry Miller has pointed out, the mere act of trying became more and more associated with a state of grace. Struggle to become converted and struggle to do good became the identifying marks of a Christian life. Thus Thomas Hooker in the seventeenth century wrote in a sermon on sin: ". . . the will of man [is] the chiefest of all [God's] workmanship, all for his body, the body of the soul, the mind to attend upon the will, the will to attend upon God and to make choice of Him and His will, that is next to Him and He only above that."[2] Urian Oakes, another New England preacher of the seventeenth century concedes that man must ultimately be considered "a poor dependent nothing-creature" unable "to move a step, or fetch his next breath . . . without help from God."[3] The race is not always to the swift, nor the battle to the strong, but usually it is: man's strength, will, perseverance are, according to Oakes, secondary causes. Yet ". . . the Lord doth most ordinarily award success unto causes of greatest sufficiency rather than disappointment and defeat."[4] In short, endeavor usually precedes accomplishment; such is God's dispensation of human affairs.

In the latter part of the eighteenth century all orthodox theology in New England was influenced by Jonathan Edwards' treatise on the freedom of the will, which became standard reading in the seminaries. Edwards argued with brilliant logic for the doctrine of election and for man's dependence on the eternal decrees of God, rather than on his own exertions in the matter of conversion and consequent salvation. In effect, Edwards took his stand on what very closely resembled simple necessity, contending that since God foreknows what men will, man is of necessity compelled to will these very things: "It is . . . evident, that if there be a full, certain, and infallible foreknowledge of the future existence of the volition of moral agents, then there is a certain infallible and indissoluble connection between those events and that foreknowledge; and that therefore . . . those events [the volitions] are necessary events. . . ."[5] To Edwards, one may will what one chooses, but what he chooses—the direction of the will—is outside his control.

Yet in no way does this extremely influential Calvinist theorist suggest that man cease to exert his will. He insists, rather, that his doctrine does not reduce man to a mere machine. "Endeavors which we use," he reasons, "are things that exist; and therefore they belong to the general chain of events; all parts of which chain are supposed to be connected; and so endeavors are supposed to be connected with some effects, or some consequent things or other. And certainly this does not hinder but that the events they are connected with, may be those we aim at, and which we choose, because we judge them most likely to have connection with those events, from the established order and course of things which we observe, or from something in Divine revelation."[6] Endeavor, then, is part of the order of things; Providence achieves its predetermined ends through the effort and struggle of the human will.

Since conversion is to a Calvinist the most important single event in a man's life, Edwards exhorted the unconverted to struggle to achieve it. Struggle cannot insure conversion, of course, but without struggle it is unlikely to occur. Hence Edwards was deeply interested in the psychology of conversion. He himself is one of those credited with sparking the Great Awakening which in the 1740's swept New England and later the other colonies with an unprecedented revivalistic fervor. By his own efforts in Northampton, Massachusetts, he brought scores of the unregenerate to the emotional pitch favorable to conversion. In his essay on the religious affections, actually a work of psychology, he depicts the fierce inner struggles, the Herculean exertions of will which precede the first regenerative breakthrough to total and overpowering faith in Christ.

III *Emerson: "In the will work and acquire"*

The great paradox of New England Protestantism, then, was that, while its basic Calvinism was deterministic, strongly minimizing man's ability to shape his own destiny by his own will, yet it actually made the will the most important human faculty. The average New Englander, moreover, was thoroughly conversant in the various theories of the will. Oliver Wendell Holmes pointed out that a churchgoing New Englander received during his lifetime the equivalent of a college education in doctrine. One of the favorite sermon topics was the will and its freedom or lack of freedom. Trained at a first-rate school like Bangor or Andover, any village minister would have been only too eager to pass on his knowledge to his congregation.

In the nineteenth century, Transcendentalist thinking about

the will had the result of enhancing the prominence already accorded it by the orthodox. Emerson's works, of course, were being read widely, especially such essays as "Self-Reliance" and "Compensation"; and Emerson was one of Miss Wilkins' "spiritual fathers."[7] The concluding passage of "Self-Reliance" exalts the human will to a level with the Godhead: "Most men gamble with [fortune] and gain all, and lose all, as her wheel rolls. But do thou leave as unlawful these winnings, and deal with Cause and Effect, the chancellors of God. In the Will work and acquire, and thou hast chained the wheel of chance. . . ." This concept appears to be the opposite of determinism.

On the other hand, in his essay on "Fate" in *The Conduct of Life* Emerson leans toward a benign determinism. Man shares in the eternal mind (the Oversoul); thus man's mind, being a particle of God's, controls the material forces of cause and effect. The individual's share in the Oversoul must be in harmony with the whole, which is obviously self-governing. Thus the individual will, when operating untrammeled, is carrying out the Divine will in which it shares. Man is free, therefore, to do the Oversoul's will. God's will and man's will are the same, and both, of course, are good. Emerson's conclusion is thus essentially the same as St. Augustine's: true freedom lies in the inability to do evil.

"He who sees through the design," writes Emerson, "presides over it, and must will that which must be. We sit and rule, and though we sleep, our dream will come to pass. Our thought, though it were only an hour old, affirms an oldest necessity, not to be separated from thought, and not to be separated from will. They must always have coexisted. . . . It is not mine or thine, but the will of all mind. It is poured into the souls of all men, as the soul itself which constitutes them men. . . . A breath of will blows eternally through the universe of souls in the direction of the Right and Necessary."[8]

Emerson's remarks are reminiscent of Jonathan Edwards' views. One "must will that which must be" sounds almost Calvinistic. So does the following from the same essay: "The tendency of every man to enact all that is in his constitution is expressed in the old belief that the efforts which we make to escape from our destiny only serve to lead us into it" (42). Paraphrased into Calvinist terms these statements mean simply that the saints, come what may, will inevitably persevere to their salvation for which they have been elected, and those who have not been elected will just as inevitably work for their own damnation. Any efforts these unfortunates make to escape their damnation will serve only to lead them into it—though their efforts are backed by the last jot of the will's energy. Finally, Emerson's statement (still in the essay on Fate) that "a man's fortunes are the fruit of his character" (41) echoes the Calvinist assumption that the elect will be righteous and prosper and the abandoned will be wicked and grow poor. "I have noticed," continues Emerson, "[that] a man likes better to be complimented on his position, as the proof of the last or total excellence, than on his merits" (42).

Thus Emerson, entangled in the perennial New England controversy over the freedom of the will, argued himself back into a position not fundamentally different from that of the strictest orthodoxy. The significant thing is that he still emphasizes the function of the will, the need for exerting it in our living, as an instrument whereby God (the Oversoul) achieves His purposes. Whether or not the will is free is not the point; Emerson emphasizes the importance of one's being true, in all endeavors involving effort of the will, to the best in one's own nature. Doing so is the equivalent of being true to God, Who *is* the best in men's natures. It involves sloughing off the encrustations of convention that coat spirits and impede their movement. To achieve release from convention and shallow conformity is the most difficult task the soul can undertake, requiring as much effort and struggle as a Puritan conversion.

From the earliest times and through the nineteenth century in New England, the will had not only been a subject of discussion but an object of cultivation. For the settlement of a wilderness, a vigorous will combined with a sense of mission (that is, a conviction that the divine will and the human will coincide in their purposes) was invaluable. The first settlements were obviously established by sheer doggedness. And the later wave of immigration that settled the hill farms and founded hundreds of backcountry villages was energized by the same irresistible will power. When Seth Hubbell, recalling his own hardships in moving his home from Connecticut to northern Vermont, marveled at the "fortitude and presence of mind I then had to bear up under them," he was honoring the qualities inculcated and nurtured by his church as the basis of all human accomplishment.

IV *An "Awful Will"*

Mary Wilkins among American writers is the supreme analyst of the Puritan will in its noble strength, in its aberrations, and in its decadence into mere whim and stubbornness. The will is the subject of scores of her stories and of all her major novels. The theme of these works is the general one that the will among the Puritans is liable to overdevelopment and can be rechanneled into useful courses only by a struggle resulting in emotional change so sudden and violent as to resemble religious conversion. The stories already discussed provide many examples of Miss Wilkins' treatment of the will, but it is worthwhile to examine one single story solely as an illustration of her ideas on the subject. Of a hundred possible stories, "A Conflict Ended" from *A Humble Romance* is typical.

In the simple plot, Marcus Woodman has strongly objected to the appointment by the village Congregational Church of a minister who is not "doctrinal." Rashly, he vows that he will spend his Sabbaths sitting on the meetinghouse steps rather than attend worship conducted by such a parson. Someone retorts that he will have to sit there fifty years then. Indeed, as the story opens, he has been sitting there summer and winter during Sunday meetings for ten years, a victim of "his awful will" (397). His fiancée, the dressmaker Esther Barney, also has a formidable will. Refusing to marry someone who is making a fool of himself —she is very sensitive to village opinion—she breaks the engagement. A strange relationship develops between the two. Far from becoming enemies, they unconsciously remain very fond of each other, despite their outer antagonism. As she enters the church each Sunday morning, Esther inquires after Marcus' mother; and, if it is sunny, she offers him the use of her parasol. Yet they can never be married unless a complete reversal occurs in the course each one is pursuing.

Esther changes first. Her young apprentice, Margy, has had a falling out with her own lover and for a time proudly refuses a reconciliation. But finally Margy humbles her pride and takes the necessary first step that restores her life to bliss. Thus is suggested to Esther that she might take the initiative in approaching Marcus. Many objections stand in the way of her decision. She is resentful of the ridicule that Marcus has brought upon himself. She is not sure that he still cares for her sufficiently to marry her. She has become so comfortably "set" in her old maid's ways that she hesitates to change them by marriage. After much inner conflict she gives in, moved by Margy's example, and tells Marcus that she will wed him even if he chooses to continue his "sit-in" on the church porch.

The will that carried her through ten years of stubborn opposition was so strong that only by a furious struggle could she overcome it. But once the reversal was achieved, she persisted in her new course with equal inflexibility. Thus the two are married. The Sunday after the wedding she and Marcus climb the church steps and Marcus hesitates:

> "Oh, Esther, I've—got—to stop."
> "Well, we'll both sit down here, then."
> "*You*?"
> "Yes; I'm willing."
> "No; you go in."
> "No, Marcus; I sit with you on our wedding Sunday."
> Her sharp, middle-aged face as she looked up at him was fairly heroic. This was all she could do: her last weapon was used. If this failed, she would accept the chances with which she had married, and before the eyes of all these tittering people she would sit down at his side on these church steps. She was determined, and she would not weaken. (397-98)

Marcus' struggle has been even more dire than hers has been. In tears he had confessed to Esther, when she offered to marry him, that his life had been a misery, that he now knows he would have given all he had to have got up any one of the Sundays in the past and walked into the church. But he has been unable to; he "ain't made strong enough to" (396). So the Sunday when the newlyweds hesitate on the church steps is critical in Marcus' life. But the reversal—the conversion, so to speak—occurs: "He stood for a moment staring into her face. He trembled so that the bystanders noticed it. He actually leaned over towards his old seat as if wire ropes were pulling him down upon it. Then he stood up straight, like a man, and walked through the church door with his wife. The people followed. Not one of them even smiled. They had felt the pathos in the comedy" (398). The change in Marcus has been complete and instantaneous. It was in this way that Miss Wilkins conceived of the operation of the New England will. Its actions had, for her, the same decisiveness and finality in daily as in religious life. By struggling for the right, the will could achieve it just as within the Puritan paradox. Though limited by God, the will was God's chief tool in achieving His end, which ought to be man's end.

V *"My old faith . . . comes back to me"*

Miss Wilkins was not the first nor the only author to analyze the functioning, both beneficent and harmful, of the New England will. Nathaniel Hawthorne in *The Scarlet Letter* had drawn the frightening portrait of Roger Chillingworth, a man whose life is devoted to the single grim volition of discovering and taking his revenge upon his wife's seducer. Chillingworth himself, in moments of insight, becomes appalled at the hold his unholy purpose has upon him and wonders if he is not acting out some predestined role and whether or not his will is not the instrument of a power greater than he is. Just as Marcus Woodman feels himself constrained by wires, so Chillingworth feels himself in a bondage outside his control. "My old faith, long forgotten," he says, "comes back to me. . . . It has all been a dark necessity." Likewise, Hollingsworth in *The Blithedale Romance* becomes so much the slave of his life's purpose of reforming criminals that he excludes from his make-up such human indispensables as tolerance, sympathy, and love. Indeed, the dehumanization of the heart that afflicts so many of Hawthorne's characters is the result of a wrongly directed but irresistible will; such is Dr. Rappaccini's fanatical devotion to science or Ethan Brand's unending search for the Unpardonable Sin.

Melville, too, addressed himself to anatomizing the perverse will. Captain Ahab is in the grip of a volition so monstrous that it engulfs not only himself but all those who come within its orbit. Ahab, like Chillingworth, considers that he is a puppet of some higher power, and like Chillingworth feels that he is fulfilling a divine purpose in eradicating evil from the world. Irresistible to others, his will is irresistible to himself. Fully able to do what he wills, he is unable to choose the ends to which his will is directed—a plight similar to that postulated by Jonathan Edwards for mankind in general: Man is free to do as he pleases but not free to please as he pleases. Thus Captain Ahab exults: "I am fate's lieutenant; I act under orders." The hero of Melville's *Pierre* also feels himself a victim of unopposable determinisms that effect his ruin and that of those dearest to him by his "free" act of will.

Of a lesser literary magnitude, but closer to Miss Wilkins in subject matter, technique and settings are Harriet Beecher Stowe and Rose Terry Cooke, both tellers of stories about New England village life. Though Miss Wilkins was unquestionably influenced by Hawthorne, it is into the tradition represented by these two women authors that she more naturally fits. In *Poganuc People*, the setting of which is the hills of northwestern Connecticut, Mrs. Stowe presents a memorable study of the overdeveloped will in her characterization of Zeph Higgins. All his life Zeph had channeled his stubborn energies into a combat with the New England soil. The owner of a thirteen-acre lot "so rocky that a sheep could scarce find a nibble there," he defied public opinion that pronounced the land worthless and fanatically set about removing every stone and placing it in a mammoth encircling wall. Year after year he proved the rightness of his efforts by growing a good crop. "And how," Mrs. Stowe asks, "would New England's rocky soil and icy hills have been made mines of wealth unless there had been human beings born to oppose, delighting to combat and wrestle, and with an unconquerable power of will."[9]

But having piled his Connecticut field stones into walls to outlast the pyramids, Zeph Higgins, like many a Wilkins character, squanders his powers in pointless quarrelsomeness. A disagreement with the Congregational deacon results in Zeph's leaving the sect to which he and his family had belonged for two hundred years and joining the Episcopal Church, the formalism of which could only be a torture to his independent nature. When the site of a district school becomes a subject of heated debate, Zeph takes matters into his own hands by yoking his oxen and dragging the schoolhouse on a sledge to the location he favors. Always a Federalist, he votes Democratic to spite his newly acquired enemies the Congregationalists, who are Federalists. If there had been a way of voting to spite both parties, Zeph would have experienced pure bliss. His actions are not determined by his own preference but by their likelihood of offending his fellow townsmen.

Small towns everywhere possess such characters, but New England back-country towns were, and are, especially productive of them. There were, in fact, almost as many forms of wrongheadedness as there were individuals of strong or stubborn nature. Lives would be wasted in miserliness, in bitter litigation with neighbors or relatives over a right of way or a boundary, in obsessive orderliness and neatness in one's housekeeping, in a monomaniacal preoccupation with the salvation of one's soul, in morbid devotion to the memory of a thwarted love, or in perpetuating a feud arising from some trivial insult. At other times, particularly in communities more in the stream of affairs, these energies would be drained off into some reform movement, such as prohibition, women's rights, or anti-vivisection. The vitality that had conquered the wilderness was now brought to bear against the real or imagined evils of the social order.

In the same vein as *Poganuc People* are the writings of Rose Terry Cooke. Her fictional Connecticut village of Bassett, the scene of many of her stories, is heavily populated with gnarled and crotchety eccentrics. Writing contemporaneously with Miss Wilkins and appearing in the same periodicals with her, she followed very much the same pattern in her stories as Miss Wilkins did. A character asserts his will unyieldingly in a wrong direction until his volition is finally broken or reversed to the accompaniment of an emotional upheaval suggestive of a religious conversion. Such a character is Freedom Wheeler in the story "Freedom Wheeler's Controversy with Providence." Freedom Wheeler is outraged against God for causing his wife to bear girls when he is desirous of having a boy upon whom he can bestow his own given name. When his wife, exhausted by the child-bearing, the browbeating, and the toil of life on a stony hill-farm, does produce a boy, the baby is so weakened by the mother's poor health that it scarcely survives its christening. After the birth of a second boy, who fares no better, the wife herself dies.

In no way chastened, Freedom marries again. A boy is soon born, but Freedom is ill at the time of the baptism and the wife names the child Tryagustus. Enraged, Freedom awaits a second boy, who arrives and is duly baptized and named after the father but is killed when Freedom trips and falls as he is carrying the infant to its mother. This shock breaks Freedom's will. Though endowed with a simple faith in the Bible as interpreted by the New England church, he at first finds little comfort in his religion; he falls into a paralyzing melancholy, asking no aid or forgiveness of God, Who he feels would justly regard his prayers as an abomination. Yet after a time he softens into a more pliable and happier person. Like Marcus Woodman, he becomes aware of the misery of his willfulness. With that realization he is soon ready to submit to the inevitable.

CHAPTER 5

Three Novels on the Will and the Conscience

I Jane Field

IN JANUARY, 1893, Mary Wilkins published in book form her first novel, the tragi-comedy *Jane Field*. It had previously been serialized in *Harper's New Monthly*, and with the final installment in November, 1892, appeared a full-page portrait of Miss Wilkins, still looking young and almost pert despite her forty years. "The Editor's Easy Chair" of the same issue contained words of praise for the novel and its author's naturalness, spontaneity, and realism. Miss Wilkins' art, the editor opined, is not the result of formal education. No one told her how to write. Not a mere recorder of observations, she transfers to her pages images generated by her fancy and her inward perceptions, much as the old balladists produced their verses. "Nothing in the history of literature stands so entirely by itself as the career of this demure New England maiden" (961).

The action of *Jane Field* begins in the back-country town of Green River, a half day by rail from Boston and obviously modeled on one of the Windham County towns near Brattleboro. The setting of the latter part of the novel is in Elliot, just outside Boston and highly suggestive of Randolph. The widow Jane Field lives with her ailing daughter Lois, whose job as teacher in the village school constitutes their sole means of support, though at such a place at that time her salary could have been no more than five dollars a week. Convinced by busybody neighbors that Lois is suffering from consumption, Mrs. Field is in despair. A letter from a lawyer in Elliot addressed to Mrs. Field's recently dead sister announces that the sister's father-in-law has left her his very substantial estate. In case the sister is not living, the inheritance goes to the daughter of another of the old man's sons.

Since Mrs. Field and her sister had always looked very much alike, Mrs. Field, a woman of granite will and purpose, decides to impersonate her sister and claim the legacy; for there is no other way to get the funds necessary to restore her daughter's health. Mrs. Field is totally an offspring of the Puritans; she attends meeting twice weekly and she is possessed of a sensitive conscience as well as of a powerful volition. Thus an elaborate rationalization precedes the imposture she is planning. She justifies her course by the fact that she had loaned her dead sister's husband a sum of $1500 that he had never paid back. She would take that sum of money and not one cent more. She concludes: ". . . everybody ought to have what's their just due . . . folks ought to lay hold of justice themselves if there ain't no other way, an' that's what we've got hands for" (33).

Thus determined, Mrs. Field sets off for Elliot where she deceives the local lawyer and the whole town, including many relatives of her sister's husband, into believing she is the rightful heir. But her first night in Elliot, alone in the big old house that is part of the inheritance, she suffers pangs of conscience. She does not go to bed but sits up in a lightless room: "Gradually this steady-headed, unimaginative old woman became possessed by a legion of morbid fancies, which played like wild fire over the terrible main fact of the case—the fact that underlay everything—that she had sinned, that she had gone over from good to evil, and given up her soul for a handful of gold" (92). For the next few months, during which she is joined by her daughter, her existence is a life-and-death struggle between her will and her sense of having made a choice for evil. To assuage her conscience, she is careful to eat none of the food that is in the house but subsists largely on berries and on eggs from chickens she has purchased. Also, she gives away many household articles to the mother of the rightful heiress. Thus her reason tells her she is doing right; she will take only the equivalent of what is justly hers and then somehow hand over the rest to the legal owner. To carry on in this painful position she brings into play her superhuman will power. "I'm a-follwin' out my own law an' my own right," she tells her daughter. "I ain't ashamed of it. If you want to be you can" (169). As Miss Wilkins says, "Although fairly started forth in the slough of deceit, she still held up her Puritan skirts arduously" (137).

According to New England theology from the seventeenth century to the end of the nineteenth, the will working alone in the presence of its creator was considered the prime mover of lives. Man must exert his will to do right, to avoid sin. Nothing worth while is accomplished except by mighty travail of the will. The harder he tries to do right, as his conscience directs, the more Godly he is. Effort itself is a sign of grace. That man is frequently confronted with conflicting objects of the will is not surprising: the Devil entices in one direction and God in another, and it is not always easy to tell which is which. But the choice must finally be made. Mrs. Field's dilemma is the classical Puritan one.

Outbursts of emotion normally accompany any act of will that sweeps one finally into a new path—say, the path of rebirth in Christ. Most Puritan divines, such as Jonathan Edwards, recognized this. It is as if the will needs a sudden last surcharge of energy to make its irreversible plunge forward. Mrs. Field has shown herself prone to such outbursts. The violent act of volition that sent her off to Elliot bent on subterfuge was preceded by an almost barbaric fit of grief for her daughter, who had been carried home after fainting on the village street. The residue of this passion encased her as in armor while she went about the execution of her plan: "Her own nature had grown so intense that it apparently had emanations, and surrounded her with an atmosphere of her own impenetrable to the world" (69). The volcanic, passional core of the outwardly restrained New England character is well illustrated in Mrs. Field.

But imposture is of course sinful; and though initially espoused by the will and sanctioned by the reason, it must ultimately be abandoned by all but the most irretrievably lost. Mrs. Field is not among the unredeemable. One summer afternoon while she is berrying, a violent thunderstorm overtakes her. The storm is an accurate reflection of the turmoil in her own soul. Arriving home, she finds three friends from Green River have arrived to see her; not knowing the desperate part she is playing, they constitute an inadvertent jeopardy to her hitherto successful impersonation. Even though a week passes without divulgence of her secret—all this is incredible to the reader—Mrs. Field is approaching the turning point. Having chosen the path of sin, she now reverses herself, and with equally merciless lashings of her will she drives herself onto the highway of repentance.

". . . Jane Field lay awake all night. Suddenly at dawn she formed a plan; her mind was settled. There was seemingly no struggle. It was to her as if she had turned a corner, once turned there was no other way, and no question about it" (248). But if her decision is taken in calmness, the volcano erupts that afternoon. Her voice rises "to a stern shriek" (259) as she informs her friends that she "ain't Esther Maxwell," her sister. Not content to confess only to her cronies, she parades up and down the street stopping the townspeople and knocking at doors to inform the world she "ain't Esther Maxwell." Here is the equivalent of conversion—the paroxysm, the remorse, the life that suddenly reverses its direction, all revealed to the eyes of the gaping public. Having seen her error in taking it on herself "to do justice instead of the Lord" (259), Mrs. Field can do no less than spend the summer informing the countryside of her sin. It is as natural an act for a Puritan as that of Judge Sewall, who after the Salem witchcraft scare had died down admitted his guilt at church before the congregation. To the New Englander for several centuries one's sins and one's repentance for them were matters of public concern. The eyes of the townspeople were as searching and as critical as those of God.

But with Mrs. Field, as with many of Mary Wilkins' characters, "the stern will of the New England woman had warped her whole nature into one groove" (266). She now *overpays* for her sin. Her state is one of psychopathy rather than of grace. All the rest of her life she continues to announce that she "ain't Mrs. Maxwell." The will has done its work all too efficiently, as it usually does with a religious melancholiac. As Foster suggests, Mrs. Field may well have been modeled after one of the inmates of the State Asylum near which the Wilkinses lived in Brattleboro. In New England where the Puritan will and conscience still lingered but where there was no adequate outlet for the energies they generated, such cases must have been quite common. A proud people nurtured in a harsh theology functions best when confronted with a challenge—a wilderness to settle, a village to settle, a village to build. When poverty and defeat engulf them, the old forces of mind and spirit become malignancies and produce grotesques.

As a story, *Jane Field* is a failure. The author too boldly violates the canons of credibility even for a novel purporting to be a romance, which *Jane Field* is not intended to be. But it is a success as a presentation of New England village life and character. Green River is the purely residual type of community found in the New England hills—a mere remnant of the teeming, hopeful settlement it once was. It has its school, its church, its town functionaries. There is even a railroad only a mile away. But if the census figures for all such towns hold true for Green River, it has now (in the novel) no more than half its population of sixty years ago. And since the farms up in the hills have been for the most part deserted, it is no longer a market center; and Mrs. Field's grinding poverty, as well as that of her friends, is typical. Neighbor is driven to meannesses against neighbor in trying to secure whatever jobs are available. Thus a school board member uses Lois's illness as a pretext to replace her as teacher by his own daughter, so necessary to him is her wretched wage. The three townswomen are able to visit Mrs. Field in Elliot only because the railroad is offering a $3.60 week's excursion to Boston. So fundless are they that they forgo their lunches between trains. The outing was indeed the great event in the lives of these mature women. One of them had never been to Boston before. Another, a housewife descended from a line of ministers, is able to absent herself only after a painful searching of her conscience: her pleasure strikes her as spiritually and materially unfeasible: " 'Well, I dunno but I've been pretty faithful, an' minded my household the way women are enjoined to in the Scriptures; mebbe it's right for me to take this little vacation,' she said, and her serious eyes were full of tears" (217).

II Pembroke: *Village Gossip*

" 'Do you see that house? . . . the one with the front windows boarded up, without any step to the front door? Well, Barney Thayer lives there all alone. He's old Caleb Thayer's son, all the son that's left; the other one died. There was some talk of his mother's whippin' him to death. She died right after, but they said afterwards that she didn't, that he run away one night, an' went slidin' downhill, an' that was what killed him; he'd always had heart trouble. I dunno; I always thought Deborah Thayer was a pretty good woman, but she was pretty set. I guess Barney takes after her. He was goin' with Charlotte Barnard years ago—I guess 'twas as much as nine or ten years ago, now—an' they were goin' to be married. She was all ready—weddin'-dress an' bonnet an' everythin'—an' this house was 'most done an' ready for them to move into; but one Sunday night Barney he went up to see Charlotte, an' he got into a dispute with her father about the 'lection, an' the old man he ordered Barney out of the house, an' Barney he went out, an' he never went in again—couldn't nobody make him. His mother she talked; it 'most killed her; an' I guess Charlotte said all she could, but he wouldn't stir a peg.

"'He went right to livin' in his new house, an' he lives there now; he ain't married, an' Charlotte ain't. She's had chances, too. Squire Payne's son, he wanted her bad'" (305-6).

Such is the plot of *Pembroke* (excepting its dénouement) as told near the end of the novel by a village gossip to a crony from a neighboring town. Miss Wilkins had first heard the story as a child, for *Pembroke* is based on an incident in her mother's family, one that was still recounted after thirty years. Even the names of several of the persons in the real situation were transferred, with some reshuffling, to characters in the book. The house in which the Wilkinses lived in Randolph had been built by Mary Wilkins' grandfather, Barnabas Lothrop, for his son Barnabas, Junior, who was to marry the local beauty Mary Thayer. But the suitor and Mary's father got into a wrangle over politics, the young man was ordered from the house never to return, and the match was broken off at the father's command. Neither man would yield, and Mary submitted to her father's will. Later Barney left town, and the unpainted house, nearer completion than in the novel, remained uninhabited for ten years. Then old Barnabas gave it to his daughter Eleanor and her husband, Warren Wilkins. Mary must have heard the story innumerable times and in much the same language as the gossip's in *Pembroke*.

When Mrs. Wilkins told the story to her daughter, she explained the obstinacy of the two men by saying it was simply their way. But Mary Wilkins apparently was dissatisfied by such a superficial diagnosis. Now years later she was living again in

Randolph, and she resorted to a more searching probing of the motivation behind the perversity to which the house was a monument. The course that her own life was taking may have sensitized her perception. Already over forty, she was still single, still living as a boarder in a friend's home. Hanson Tyler had been a sustaining hope, and she may have been waiting for him as many of her fictional old maids waited for their absent and procrastinating lovers. But if she were waiting for Tyler, her waiting was doomed to disappointment; her own life story was not to be given a happy ending. In 1892 word came that Tyler had married in California. For some years Mary had been making extended visits in and near New York City, especially at Metuchen, New Jersey, in the household of Henry M. Alden, the editor of *Harper's New Monthly*, to which she had contributed many stories. During one of her sojourns with the Aldens at about this time, she met the man whom she was to marry eight years later. This was the hard-drinking, gay-living, horse-fancying Dr. Charles Freeman. Though holding a degree from the College of Physicians and Surgeons in New York, Dr. Freeman ran a coal and lumber business instead of practicing medicine. So strong was the attraction between him and the still-pretty middle-aged author that friends began to speculate concerning an engagement.

III Pembroke: *Purposes*

In the "Introductory Sketch" to a so-called "Biographical Edition" of *Pembroke* published by Harper in 1899, Miss Wilkins gives her most extensive statement of her views not only on this novel but on her writing in general. As this edition is extremely rare, her remarks deserve quotation in full:

> *Pembroke* was originally intended as a study of the human will in several New England characters, in different phases of disease and abnormal development, and to prove, especially in the most marked case, the truth of a theory that its cure depended entirely upon the capacity of the individual for a love which could rise above all considerations of self, as Barnabas Thayer's love for Charlotte Barnard finally did.
>
> While Barnabas Thayer is the most pronounced exemplification of this theory, and while he, being drawn from life, originally suggested the scheme of the study, a number of the other characters, notably Deborah Thayer, Richard Alger, and Cephas Barnard, are instances of the same spiritual disease. Barnabas to

me was as much the victim of disease as a man with curvature of the spine; he was incapable of straightening himself to his former stature until he had laid hands upon a more purely unselfish love than he had ever known, through his anxiety for Charlotte, and so raised himself to his own level.

When I make use of the term abnormal, I do not mean unusual in any sense. I am far from any intention to speak disrespectfully or disloyally of those stanch old soldiers of the faith who landed upon our inhospitable shores and laid the foundation, as on a very rock of spirit, for the New England of to-day; but I am not sure, in spite of their godliness, and their noble adherence, in the face of obstacles, to the dictates of their consciences, that their wills were not developed past the reasonable limit of nature. What wonder is it that their descendants inherit this peculiarity, though they may develop it for much less worthy and more trivial causes than the exiling themselves for a question of faith, even the carrying-out of personal and petty aims and quarrels?

There lived in a New England village, at no very remote time, a man who objected to the painting of the kitchen floor, and who quarrelled furiously with his wife concerning the same. When she persisted, in spite of his wishes to the contrary, and the floor was painted, he refused to cross it to his dying day, and always, to his great inconvenience, but probably to his soul's satisfaction, walked around it.

A character like this, holding to a veriest trifle with such a deathless cramp of the will, might naturally be regarded as a notable exception to a general rule; but his brethren who sit on church steps during services, who are dumb to those whom they should love, and will not enter familiar doors because of quarrels over matters of apparently no moment, are legion. *Pembroke* is intended to portray a typical New England village of some sixty years ago, as many of the characters flourished at that time, but villages of a similar description have existed in New England at a much later date, and they exist to-day in a very considerable degree. There are at the present time many little towns in New England along whose pleasant elm or maple shaded streets are scattered characters as pronounced as any in Pembroke. A short time since a Boston woman recited in my hearing a list of seventy-five people in the very small Maine village in which she was born and brought up, and every one of the characters which she mentioned had some almost incredibly marked physical or mental characteristic.

However, this state of things—this survival of the more prominent traits of the old stiff-necked ones, albeit their necks were stiffened by their resistance of the adversary—can necessarily be known only to the initiated. The sojourner from cities for the summer months cannot often penetrate in the least, though he may not be aware of it, the reserve and dignified aloofness of the dwellers in the white cottages along the road over which he drives. He often looks upon them from the superior height of a wise and keen student of character, he knows what he thinks of them, but he never knows what they think of him or themselves. Unless he is a man of the broadest and most democratic tendencies, to whom culture and the polish of society is as nothing beside humanity, and unless he returns, as faithfully as the village birds to their nests, to his summer home year after year, he cannot see very far below the surfaces of villages of which Pembroke is typical. Quite naturally, when the surfaces are broken by some unusual revelation of a strongly serrate individuality, and the tale thereof is told at his dinner-table with an accompaniment of laughter and exclamation-points, he takes that case for an isolated and by no means typical one, when, if the truth were told, the village windows are full of them as he passes by.

However, this state of things must necessarily exist, and has existed, in villages which, like Pembroke, have not been brought much in contact with outside influences, and have not been studied or observed at all by people not of their kind by birth or long familiarity. In towns which have increased largely in population, and have become more or less assimilated with a foreign element, these characters do not exist in such a large measure, are more isolated in reality, and have, consequently, less claim to be considered types. But there have been, and are to-day in New England, hundreds of villages like Pembroke, where nearly every house contains one or more characters so marked as to be incredible, though a writer may be prevented, for obvious reasons, from mentioning names and proving facts.

There is often to a mind from the outside world an almost repulsive narrowness and a pitiful sordidness which amounts to tragedy in the lives of such people as those portrayed in *Pembroke*, but quite generally the tragedy exists only in the comprehension of the observer and not at all in that of the observed. The pitied would meet pity with resentment; they would be full of wonder and wrath if told that their lives were narrow, since they have never seen the limit of the breadth of their current of daily life. A singing-school is as much to them as a symphony concert and grand opera to their city brethren, and a sewing church sociable as an afternoon tea. Though the standard of taste of the simple villagers, and their complete satisfaction therewith, may reasonably be lamented, as also their restricted view of life, they are not to be pitied, generally speaking, for their unhappiness in consequence. It may be that the lack of unhappiness constitutes the real tragedy.

IV Pembroke: *A Gallery of Grotesques–Barnabas*

In *Pembroke* Mary Wilkins presents a gallery of grotesques comparable to that in Sherwood Anderson's *Winesburg, Ohio,* which not only in its preoccupation with village-spawned abnormalities but also in style resembles Miss Wilkins' work more closely than any critic has yet noted. Barnabas, however, is probably the most spectacular and the most painstakingly explored. To begin with, Cephas Barnard, the man against whom Barnabas is pitted, is by no means a formidable adversary. Cephas is certainly stubborn and "set" in his ways, and given to making horrendous threats–which he usually backs down from. A militant vegetarian, he browbeats himself and his family into eating sorrel pies, but this is as far as his despotism goes. His wife is more than a match for him, as is his daughter. The villagers regard him as a harmless eccentric. His theories about subduing one's animal passions by abstaining from meat and warding off rheumatism by drinking gallons of water are laughable. Had Barnabas apologized two days after the argument, Cephas would have received him again as a visitor to his house and as the betrothed of his daughter. In fact Cephas, soon regretting the pain he had caused Charlotte by quarreling with her lover, goes to Barnabas himself in an endeavor to bring him back but is rebuffed.

What is the cause of Barnabas' perversity? One thing is certain. He is not swayed by public opinion, by "what people will say," that merciless censor of the actions of all but the stoutest-hearted villagers. Village opinion weighs oppressively on the conduct of most of the people in the book, but not on Barnabas. Miss Wilkins is careful to inform the reader that he is so aloof that he knows little and cares less about what people think. So he does not persist in his obduracy simply because he is afraid of being laughed at. The reason he does not apologize to Cephas and win back Charlotte, whom he still loves and who still loves him, is that *it does not occur to him that he could do so.* Miss Wilkins states this explicitly and goes on to give the reasons for

Barnabas' singular blindness. Just before his dismissal from the Barnard house, he had been on the pinnacle of a happiness so ecstatic that he could attribute it only to God's grace. Now in his abysmal unhappiness he sees the same Providence at work: "His natural religious bent, inherited from generations of Puritans, and kept in its channel by his training from infancy, made it impossible for him to conceive of sympathy or antagonism in its fullest sense apart from God" (18). The crushing of his happiness seems "to him settled and inevitable" (19), in other words, predestined; and all he can do is to exert his will in harmony with what he conceives of as God's will.

Of all Miss Wilkins' books *Pembroke* has been most often compared to Hawthorne's. Barnabas, indeed, is the most Hawthornesque of her characters. When Roger Chillingworth has been pursuing his revenge for years, he admits to Hester that he could not desist now if he wished. His course seems inevitable; his helplessness in its grip renews his belief in the fatalism of his Calvinistic faith: he is acting according to what God has predestined. Similarly, Barnabas considers himself helpless in the toils of his obsession which (like Chillingworth's hunched back) has caused his spine to bend unnaturally in correspondence with his crooked will.

> "Have you hurt your back?" [asks an acquaintance who has been startled by a resemblance between Barney and a congenital cripple hobbling down the road.]
> "I've hurt my soul," said Barney. "It happened that Sunday night years ago. I—can't get over it. I am bent like his back."
> "I should think you'd better get over it. . . ."
> "I—can't . . ." (297).

From the first, in fact, Charlotte realizes that Barney is helpless, that he has "a terrible will that won't always let him do what he wants to himself" (68). He does as he wills, but he cannot will as he chooses—a perfect example of Jonathan Edwards' thesis. Barnabas himself struggles to break his own distorted resolution. When he learns that Squire Payne's son is courting Charlotte, he can hardly endure the thought of losing her, which he considers a certainty. In one of the revolts against his fate—a rebelliousness that Miss Wilkins finds latent in the strait-jacketed New England soul—he flings himself on the ground in a convulsive grief, groaning, and sobbing, and tearing up handfuls of grass.

Barnabas has been helpless from the start. His life becomes an allegory of the dehumanized heart, as do the lives of the fanatics in Hawthorne and in Melville. The day after Barnabas breaks his engagement, he moves into his unfinished house—which now serves as a symbol of his own incomplete personality—and boards up most of the windows, thus shutting himself off physically and spiritually from human society. The curvature gradually becomes more noticeable in his spine until one winter he is bent double by a wracking attack of rheumatism brought on by frenzied woodchopping in a swamp. Through weeks of cold and snow and fierce winds that kept other men huddled at their hearths, Barney battled with the forest, itself symbolic of the Puritan heritage: "He stood from morning until night hewing down the trees, which had gotten their lusty growth from the graves of their own kind. Their roots were sunken deep among and twined about the very bones of their fathers which helped make up the rich frozen soil of the great swamp" (312).

Finally, as the villagers predicted, Barnabas becomes ill with rheumatic fever—the culmination of his spiritual sickness as well as of his physical exhaustion. Charlotte insists on nursing him despite the remonstrances of her family, who fear that her reputation will be compromised by her living alone in the house with the sick man. Though he realizes he does not deserve these attentions from one whom he has so bitterly wronged, he is still too aloof from humankind to understand that Charlotte is laying herself open to the most vicious gossip. Then one day the minister and deacon call at his house and ask to speak with Charlotte. It flashes through his mind that the church is about to take action against her. This realization of the existence of a social order is his first step back into the warmth of normal life. He orders Charlotte to go home, and she unwillingly complies. When she leaves, he once more brings his "terrible will" into play—this time to undo the damage it had previously done. If his volition had twisted his body, it could now straighten it. In physical agony he rises from his chair and forces himself to stand erect. Then he fights his way step by step to Charlotte's house. Finally, he "stood before them all with that noble bearing which comes from humility itself when it has fairly triumphed. . . . And Barney entered the house with his old sweetheart and his old self" (329-30).

It will always be a question whether Barney's change of heart is plausible. Each reader must decide for himself, but he should recall certain facts. Barney does have an "old," that is, a different self, which the reader glimpses vividly in an incident in Chapter I. He has walked into a spring evening that is fragrant with apple blossoms and pellucid with the threat, ominous perhaps, of frost. He is on his way to see Charlotte, and he stops for a moment at the nearly completed house where she will live with him: "The tears came into his eyes; he stepped forward, laid his smooth boyish cheek against a partition wall . . . , and kissed it. It was a fervent demonstration, not towards Charlotte alone, nor the joy to come to him within those walls, but to all life and love and nature, although he did not comprehend it" (7). Furthermore, Miss Wilkins does state that Barnabas' transformation is the result of a newly found humility. Now the compulsion that had caused him to reject Charlotte and board himself up in his unfinished house had originated with humiliated pride. Humiliation exacerbates pride and generates self-lacerating impulses—or at least so think Gide and Dostoyevsky. The pattern is one already seen in Miss Wilkins' writing: humility, the negation of pride, releases one from the clutches of a perverted, self-destructive will. Humility itself is generated by selfless love. In her introduction, Miss Wilkins has announced that *Pembroke* is designed to demonstrate that the diseased will can be cured only by "a love which could rise above all consideration of self." It was exactly at the point where Barnabas was able to care more about Charlotte's sacrifice of her good name for him than about his own wounded pride that he was able to redirect his will away from self and thus effect his bodily and spiritual cure.

It has been said that even the most distorted wills in Miss Wilkins' fiction exert themselves in accomplishing what their possessors think is right. I believe this is an erroneous generalization. Barnabas frequently realizes that what he is doing is wrong, but he cannot help himself. At times he tries to make material restitution to Charlotte in the form of gifts (which she refuses), for he has become wealthy in his life of solitary and frenzied labor. Like Hawthorne and Melville, Miss Wilkins is aware of the capacity for evil latent in every person's make-up.

She has a clear and Puritan vision of the power of darkness that Melville found so akin to the concept of original sin. But it is of course possible for a volition to change from the willing of evil to the willing of good, as happens with Barnabas with a somewhat disconcerting suddenness.

It is also possible for a will to be directed not only toward what one thinks is right but toward what is intrinsically right. This is the case with Charlotte, who is as beautiful and pure in soul as she is in body. The night Barney quarrels with her father she follows her lover into the street and calls after him, even when her father orders her back. Though she feels the humiliation of rejection, she slowly recovers from it. No longer smarting from her own hurt, she is able to understand the structure of Barnabas' ailment and feel compassion for him. She goes to his house to try to reason with him, not abjectly, but to help him, as well as herself. When she caresses him at the time of his mother's death and later when she nurses him in his illness, she dismisses the objections of her parents and their fears of what people will say with the simple assertion: "I am doing what I think is right" (324). Rightness is more important to her than self. Her love of Barnabas is based on love of goodness. This love regenerates his moribund "old self" and brings about his conversion to selflessness.

V *A Gallery of Grotesques: Deborah Thayer*

To understand Barnabas thoroughly one must know his mother, Deborah Thayer, whose portrait is perhaps the most astonishing in this gallery of nineteenth-century Puritans. Deborah, aptly named after the warrior prophetess of the Old Testament, is presented through a remarkable series of similes, metaphors, and analogies. As she listened to her husband reading one of the imprecatory psalms "her eyes gleamed with warlike energy . . . : she confused King David's enemies with those people who crossed her own will" (3). When she learned that her son Barnabas had jilted Charlotte, she was outraged that she declared she would "be jest as hard on him as the Lord for it" (58). "Deborah never yielded to any of the vicissitudes of life; she met them in fair fight like enemies, and vanquished them, not with trumpet and spear, but with daily duties. It was a village story how Deborah Thayer cleaned all the windows in the house one afternoon when her first child had died in the morning" (95-96). When she and her son met after the break with Charlotte, "the two faces confronted each other in silence, while it was as if two wills clashed swords in advance of them" (103). She spooned out gravy into a bowl "as if it were molten lead instead of milk; . . . she might . . . have been one of her female ancestors in the times of the French and Indian Wars, casting bullets with the yells of savages in her ears . . ." (146). She administered medicine in a spoon to her sick son Ephraim "as if it were a bayonet and there were death at the point" (221-22). In her grief when her son died, her face worked "like the breaking up of an icy river" (247).

The fact is that Deborah at times confuses herself with God; always she is assured that her will is His. In her own household she is a wrathful tyrant, just as God, in her view, is a wrathful tyrant in his Heaven. She has banished Barnabas, her equal in will power, from the house. She opposes her daughter's love affair with a local boy until the girl has intercourse with him, becomes pregnant, is ordered from her home in a howling blizzard, and is married under duress to her lover in the home of the village whore, who alone among the townspeople has had the decency to take her in out of the snow. Most implacable is Deborah's domination over her younger son, Ephraim, a boy afflicted with serious heart disease. Deborah's theology is that of the Westminster Assembly of the mid-seventeenth century, the catechism of which was the basic document in New England Puritanism. Deborah accepts its Calvinistic doctrines without demur and regards herself as one of its most faithful supporters and propagators. Ephraim is so ill bodily that the doctor has forbidden him all normal boyish play and has cautioned against rich foods and corporal punishment. Yet Deborah considers it her duty to drum the catechism mercilessly into him, despite his precarious health, for she believes the immortal soul is more important than the mortal body. Her duty, dictated directly by God, is to make Ephraim learn his catechism; and Ephraim does learn it, even to the extent of developing a conviction that he himself is one of the elect.

But for all the Lord's grace Ephraim is on the whole miserable. One day he rebels against God and his mother. He sneaks out of the house at night and joins another boy in coasting down a hill. Ephraim's release is a glorious one. He shouts deliriously as his sled races down the slope, and he beats his friend in speed and in distance. It is the one time in his life that he acts like a boy, and it is also the end of his life. The exertion, as well as an entire mince pie he has stolen from the larder the same night and consumed, combine to give him his death sickness. Moreover, his mother, who does not yet know of the sledding party, whips him for another offence. Against the physician's orders, she thinks the punishment necessary if the child's soul is to be saved: ". . . it was a high purpose to Deborah Thayer. She did not realize the part which her own human will had in it. . . . 'Ephraim,' said his mother, 'I have spared the rod with you all my life because you were sick. Your brother and your sister have both rebelled against the Lord and against me" (239). As she applies the rod with vigor, Ephraim dies.

Even as he dies under the scourge of her hand and her will, she prays over his corpse "a strange prayer, full of remorse, of awful agony, of self-defense of her own act, and her own position as the vicar of God upon earth for her child" (240). She declares to Jehovah that she would have laid Ephraim on the altar as Abraham laid Isaac. She prays most of her waking hours for nearly a year: "Deborah had not the least doubt that she had killed her son . . ." (245). Her problem is to square her will with God's. Gossip becomes menacing. There is talk of the church's taking action against her. Then one day Ephraim's companion divulges the story of the clandestine sledding party. While thanking the Lord for letting her know that she perhaps had not killed her son, Deborah herself falls dead of heart failure.

Deborah's faith is old-time Calvinist orthodoxy in its most rigid form. As Edwards says, one wills what God wills one to will —and it must please man to will thus in harmony with God. It is inappropriate to apply modern psychological theory to the action and motivation of the characters in *Pembroke*, written in 1894; Miss Wilkins knew nothing about present theories of the unconscious mind. But she did know much about Calvinism, and what she knew both fascinated and repelled her. Her own religion was one of love, a Protestantism softened by the social gospel and the humanitarianism of the times. Yet through observation and from countless tales she had heard of the eccentricities of New England villagers, she knew something about the relationship of pride and humiliation, especially when modified by the strong will which the regional religion encouraged. From these materials and from the doctrines of her forebears she spun the rural tragedies of her best work and pointed to *agape* and humility as the solvent for the glacial rigidity of lives frozen by pride and wrath. Her psychology, though not Freudian or belonging to any other school of today, is a respectable one; and it is convincing within the world of her fiction.

VI *"Not a Summer Vacation"*

Pembroke is Miss Wilkins' finest novel, and in her own day it won enthusiastic acclaim. Conan Doyle pronounced it the best novel written in America since *The Scarlet Letter*. E. A. Robinson, reading it in Gardiner, Maine, a town in which Miss Wilkins would have felt herself no stranger, declared that the book was true to New England as he knew it. Robinson, however, was not an uncritical admirer of Mary Wilkins. The "Pastels in Prose," which she wrote for the December, 1892, *Harper's*, he described accurately as drool. Imitations of a French genre then in vogue, these word miniatures on such subjects as "Camilla's Snuff Box," and "Death" are mere verbal bric-a-brac. But to Robinson, *Pembroke* was quite another matter; and his words in a letter to Harry De Forest Smith, written October 28, 1894 (the year the novel was published), stand today as its outstanding appreciation. To Robinson, *Pembroke* was "strange in its very simplicity. Everything is drawn against a tragic background of subdued passion and some of the scenes are almost magnificent in their treatment. To the careless modern reader the plot—or rather the plots—will seem impossible and contrary to human nature; but to one who knows anything about Puritanism the book will be interesting and impressive. Narrow-minded and unsympathetic readers had better keep away from it. It is a rather significant fact that it finds more appreciation in England than America. . . ."[1]

Robinson then says that he admires Miss Wilkins for "treating some things so openly." In referring to "a few animal touches that are hardly like anything else that I have ever seen in novels" (175), he probably has in mind the events preceding Barney's sister's "shotgun" marriage—almost the norm for marriages in small New England villages during the past hundred years or so—and to the description of the village whore at whose house the wedding was performed. Robinson praises the style of the book as "eminently qualified for reading aloud. It never drags for a page and is always either bright or gloomy. Although it 'ends well' in a way, *Pembroke* life is not a summer vacation. It is pretty much like any other life,—that is, relatively" (175). In *Pembroke* Robinson was probably seeing much of his own town of Gardiner, where life also was proving to be far from a summer vacation. His own first poems, soon to appear, dealing with Tilbury Town, as he called Gardiner, evoke the same somber background he finds in Miss Wilkins' novel. The satanic kinks that bedevil so many of the Tilbury citizens resemble the diseased wills of Miss Wilkins' characters. In both cases the defects, which exert a somewhat deterministic influence, are presented as the inevitable outcroppings of the village environment and its moribund tradition.

Pembroke is all that Robinson says it is. It is true to New England life, as true as the works of Hawthorne and of Emily Dickinson. With its indigenous Biblical names and its numerous Scriptural allusions, *Pembroke* catches the spirit of the Old Testament theocracy that still lingered ghostlike in New England. In the characterization of Barnabas, and perhaps of Deborah, it achieves tragic catharsis—the exhibition of strong persons brought low by the flaw of *hubris*. In Charlotte is a calm unswerving strength that is rooted in a deep sense of her own and others' intrinsic worth. Her steadfast acceptance of life and her eventual triumph of forgiveness over all personal and public pettiness remind one of Hester Prynne as she went about her daily life in seventeenth-century Boston. In her ability through inner strength to rise above circumstances through personal suffering, she represents the highest type of tragic heroine.

The present neglect of *Pembroke* is difficult to understand. Studies of the New England conscience, in both its past and present manifestations, are perennially popular. Analyses of mental illnesses, "realistic" studies of poverty and degradation, probings of the problem of evil—all of which *Pembroke* contains in abundance—are the essentials of twentieth-century fiction. Nor is the book "Victorian" in its treatment of sex. It is true to the sexual mores of the time, but these mores in rural New England were much laxer than is generally imagined. Finally, as

Robinson points out, *Pembroke* is written in a clear, forceful style, with terse dialogue as befits the tight-lipped village speakers, and with many evocative but brief descriptions of landscape and weather, weddings and funerals, and all the daily routine that lurks like a chorus behind any village tragedy.

VII Madelon

Miss Wilkins believed that in every New England village some crime or sinister secret lay hidden—a view that suggests Hawthorne's preoccupation with secret guilt in all his major novels and in such stories as "Young Goodman Brown" and "The Minister's Black Veil." The presence of hidden sin in any community or family would be taken for granted, of course, in an even moderately Calvinistic outlook. A belief in original sin—or "something, somehow like Original Sin," as Melville puts it in regard to Hawthorne's view of life—makes such an assumption virtually inevitable.

In Miss Wilkins' *Madelon*, brought out by Harper in 1896, the village of Ware Centre, Vermont, is the scene of a stabbing that almost takes a man's life. The assailant is Madelon Hautville, a high-spirited, dark-haired girl of French and Indian ancestry diluted by marriages for several generations into Yankee families. The victim is Lot Gordon, a sickly, bookish man hopelessly in love with Madelon. Madelon herself is in love with Lot's cousin Burr, who has jilted her for a golden-haired Anglo-Saxon girl, Dorothy Fair, daughter of the orthodox parson. One night, as Madelon is returning from a dance where Burr has made evident his preference for Dorothy, Lot in desperation accosts her on the dark woods road and attempts to kiss her. Mistaking him for his cousin, she stabs him with a knife that her brother Richard has lent her to drive off bears. Lot falls, badly hurt but not dead. Running back to the village for help, Madelon meets Burr, tells him what has happened, and takes him back to the wounded man. Other merrymakers from the dance approach along the road. Burr successfully urges Madelon to return home. He remains behind. Richard, who has been following his sister to make sure she gets home safely, comes up; Burr Gordon gives him back his bloody knife, first wiping it on the snow. Burr then lays his own in its place in the pool of blood from Lot's wound. The merrymakers arrive on the scene, and Burr is incriminated beyond all reasonable doubt. He is arrested and placed in the county jail.

Madelon confesses to the assault, but no one believes her. It has been pointed out that her position is somewhat like Raskolnikov's, who is not believed when he confesses to murder. Miss Wilkins in fact had recently read *Crime and Punishment*, of which she said: "I am at odds with the whole thing, but it is a wonderful book. [Dostoyevsky] writes with more concentrated force than Tolstoy. This book seems to me like one of my own nightmares, and told on my nerves."[2] But the resemblance between *Madelon* and *Crime and Punishment* is slight. Madelon has committed a crime of passion, not one of intellectual premeditation, like Raskolnikov's. Nor does Madelon attempt to conceal her guilt. From the beginning she is bent on confessing; and when she learns that Burr, whom she still loves, is in jail for her crime, she becomes "nothing but a purpose concentrated upon one end; there was in her that great impetus of the human will which is above all the swift forces of the world when once it is aroused" (115).

In other words, *Madelon* is another of Miss Wilkins' explorations of the potentialities of the will. Madelon herself is presented as a combination of passion stemming from her "savage" forebears and of Calvinistic conscience and pertinacity traceable to the New England strain in her heritage. She has all the sense of duty, the singlemindedness of Miss Wilkins' most willful characters. She differs from a "pure-blooded" New Englander only in her fiery temperament, which Miss Wilkins associated with dark-haired Indians and the French rather than with the fair-haired Anglo-Saxons. Madelon, then, is an example of the dark heroine whose malignity, as Harry Levin has pointed out, was so commonly contrasted in nineteenth-century fiction with the benignity of blue-eyed blondes, for example, in Hawthorne's *Blithedale Romance* and Melville's *Pierre*. But Madelon is a member of Parson Fair's orthodox Congregational Church and has a mother and grandmother of English descent. The passion contributed by the "darkness" of her foreign blood when tempered with English restraint and Calvinistic theology produces a thrust of purpose not to be resisted. Poor Dorothy Fair, daughter of the Puritans though she is, is passive in contrast, despite the fact that she has the strength of will to defy her father and refuse to marry Burr.

Madelon is not successfully characterized. The explanation of her behavior in terms of her heredity is unconvincing and unnecessary. Girls of Anglo-Saxon stock elsewhere in Miss Wilkins' work display equal powers of will, a similar propensity for holding themselves "to duty, like a knife to a grindstone" (*Madelon*, 248), and for equally passionate outbursts of emotion. Miss Wilkins' ventures into anthropology and ethnology are pathetically silly. Madelon is most credible when Miss Wilkins forgets her lineage and presents her simply as a village girl of strong feelings in a situation that challenges human capacities to the utmost. When Madelon walks ten miles to the county jail on the coldest day within living memory in an attempt to free her lover of the charge of murder, she takes on a heroic grandeur that she lacks elsewhere; for she is here presented not as a combination of hereditary forces but only as a woman of strong conscience and a sense of duty, and with a lover's selflessness. The irrelevant ramifications of her family tree no longer obtrude.

The reader's impression of Madelon's passion, moreover, is enhanced by "the terrible rigor and tension of the cold" (144), which has shut down on the lonely terrain and the little lost villages like a granite lid, threatening to stiffle the breath of life of all who venture from their hearths. Indeed, Miss Wilkins' outstanding achievement in the book is her evocation of the starkness of the long Vermont winter in which most of the action is laid: the terror of a sub-zero night when house timbers creak and crack as much from the cold as from the battering northwester, the two-day blizzard with its aftermath of gales that move the snow "across the fields in great diamond-glittering shafts" (201), the sudden thaw—like the melting of the congealed wills of some of her characters—when the air is "full of the sounds of running water, of sweet, interrupted tinkles and sudden gurgles and steady outpourings as from a thousand pitchers" (229).

With equal success Mary Wilkins sketches in the background of village society, "sunken in the monotony and isolation of a Vermont country winter" (173). But the gossip, suspicion, and meddlesomeness are not seasonal; for Ware Centre, summer and winter, is not far removed in spirit from witch-hunting

Salem: "That black atmosphere of suspicion and hatred, which gathers nowhere more easily than in a New England town, was thick around Burr and Madelon. They breathed, though as yet it was in less degree, the same noxious air as did the persecuted Quakers and witches of bygone times" (334). Later, suspicion and hatred give rise to the spirit of "righteous retribution which finds easy birth in New England villages" (358), and threats are made against the persons of Madelon and Burr. In her depiction of the townspeople as a group, Miss Wilkins betrays her own conviction in something very like original sin. She writes: "The gases which lie at the bottom of human souls, which gossip and suspicious imagination upstir, are deadlier than those at the bottoms of old wells" (334). The human mind, she believes, has a tendency "born of involuntary self-knowledge which leads it to suspect a selfish motive in all untoward actions" (207).

Among the characters other than Madelon, Burr Gordon is most interesting because of the conversion-like change of heart that he undergoes. Much of the action in the book rises from the fact that Burr is actually in love with two women—the dark-haired Madelon and the golden-haired Dorothy Fair. Perhaps Miss Wilkins intended an allegory on the two aspects of women that attract men—mysterious, often destructive passionateness; and open, innocuous prettiness. Burr is torn between the two Ware Centre girls; Miss Wilkins, who states her belief that men love woman in general rather than a woman in particular, finds his dilemma a natural one. The final and conclusive weighting of Burr's love toward Madelon occurs in church the Sunday after he has been jilted at his wedding by the timorous Dorothy.

Burr had been willing to shoulder the blame for Lot's stabbing in order to save Madelon. Yet he had been ready enough to marry Dorothy. Now in church he listens to Madelon while she sings "the old orthodox hymns" with all the beauty and passion of her superb voice. Though the novel abounds in sentimental passages, this is not one of them. Burr and Madelon are no more than conventionally religious; they are not in the least pious or sanctimonious. Yet important in the context of their lives has been Parson Fair's church, which both attend regularly and in which Madelon sings in the choir. The change in Burr is not a religious conversion, but it is the psychological equivalent of one. Madelon's voice and the words and notes of the old hymns release the "love and force which are at the roots of things for the strengthening of the world. . . . When Madelon Hautville stopped singing not one in the meeting house had seen Burr Gordon stir, but the soul in him had surely turned and faced about with a great rending as of swathing wills that bound it" (317-18).

VIII *The Chain of Self-Sacrifice*

The strong point of *Madelon* is descriptive accuracy. It has interest and value as a study of New England village life; as a novel, it is not a success, and Miss Wilkins knew it. The weakness results from her trying to cram too much between two covers: realistic reporting on village life, several romantic love affairs, and physical violence. The "local color" is Miss Wilkins' authentic best. She injected the violence, perhaps, because of the success she had achieved with a detective story based loosely on the Lizzie Borden murder case, "The Long Arm," which she had written in 1895 in collaboration with J. E. Chamberlin, a columnist for the *Boston Evening Transcript*, and which won a $2,000 prize from the Bacheller Syndicate. If violence was so rewarding in one story, why not try it in another? The idea is logical, given characters in whom violence is latent and not too far beneath the surface. But Madelon, for all her Indian "blood" with which Miss Wilkins has endowed her to make her murderousness seem plausible, is not otherwise portrayed as a potential killer.

The romantic and sentimental love motif is even more of an incongruity. As Miss Wilkins had already demonstrated in scores of short stories and novels, courtship and marriage in New England villages are not carried on according to the formulae of the standard popular fiction of the day. One such formula had been succinctly stated, and rejected as spurious, by W. D. Howells in *The Rise of Silas Lapham*. The guests at a dinner party are discussing a recent novel, *Tears, Idle Tears*, in which a girl refuses to marry a man whom she loves, and who loves her, because her sister is in love with the same man and had mistakenly thought he returned her feeling. Through sacrifice of her own and her lover's happiness, the heroine thinks she will somehow assuage her sister's sorrow. Thus she refuses to marry the man who by all logic should be her husband.

As Howells points out, the result is simply to make three people miserable instead of one. Such arrangements either in fiction or in real life were, said Howells, silly, harmful, and downright immoral; since in reality people do not generally act so artificially, serious fiction should avoid such solutions. In *The Rise of Silas Lapham* the situation arises in the relationships of Irene and Penelope Lapham and the Boston blue-blood, Tom Corey. The sisters, who have been reading too many romantic novels, prepare themselves for heart-rending self-sacrifice. But the Lapham family is of Vermont origin with a lot of stern common sense, and with the advice of a sensible minister the right couple marries.

It is exactly this brand of sentimentality that Miss Wilkins has chosen to impose on her story of Ware Centre, Vermont. Self-sacrifice runs rampant. Burr attempts to sacrifice his life by assuming the blame for the stabbing of Lot, who for a long time is expected to die from the wound. Second, Lot, by swearing that his injury is the result of attempted suicide, sacrifices his reputation to free Burr in order to please Madelon. In return for this act, he exacts a promise from Madelon that she will marry him; but later he self-sacrificially releases her from the promise so that she can marry as she wishes. In the meanwhile, Madelon sacrifices herself by insisting that Burr marry Dorothy Fair; and Eugene Hautville, one of Madelon's brothers, who also loves Dorothy, sacrifices his feelings so that she can marry Burr, whom he hates. Only Dorothy's brainless fear that Burr actually is a murderer causes her not to go through with the marriage, and thus the chain of self-sacrifice is broken and the weddings which should have occurred long ago are finally celebrated. Even for a nineteenth-century audience, this fare apparently was too heady, for the book was received coldly.

CHAPTER 6

Local Color

IN ANTHOLOGIES and literary histories Mary Wilkins Freeman has usually been classified as a local colorist. Unfortunately "local color" is as vague and meaningless a term as "romanticism," "realism," or "naturalism." Hamlin Garland unintentionally reduced the concept to absurdity when he branded as local color all literature that conveys a feeling for place or period. Thus the *Iliad* is a work of local color since the description of Achilles' shield provides a picture of life in all its aspects in ancient Greece. In attempting to place Miss Wilkins in a literary tradition, then, one should discard this catch-all term and examine some writing, both fiction and criticism, that might have had an appreciable influence upon her or formed the taste for which she wrote.

I *"The plainer and commoner the better"*

There has always been among American writers an interest in the local peculiarities, the scenery, and the history of their native regions. What Irving started, Cooper, Hawthorne, and Longfellow, among the major writers, continued. The search was for a past and a distinctive heritage of manners and values that could be used as the material for literary works. American writers consistently bewailed the lack of such material in their own country; and some gave up, either temporarily or permanently, and went abroad in search of it. But others remained and doggedly worked their native mines.

Rural New England had always been of interest to readers and writers throughout the country. Timothy Dwight in *Travels in New England and New York* (1821) gave an account of the remotest townships of the area; there followed a spate of books on the life and the scenic splendors of New England, and such books have continued to appear to the present day. In fiction, the vogue for New England settings began with Catherine Sedgwick and included such famous figures as Hawthorne, Melville, James, and Howells, as well as a number of lesser ones like Harriet Beecher Stowe, Sarah Orne Jewett, Rowland Robinson, Rose Terry Cooke, and T. W. Higginson.

Typical among the literary promoters of the New England countryside, and extremely influential, especially among the women authors, was John Greenleaf Whittier, who exploited in his ballads and other narrative and descriptive poems the same kind of material from farm and village life as the fiction writers used. By birth and upbringing, Whittier was at home in the New England countryside, as were Sarah Orne Jewett, Rowland Robinson, H. B. Stowe, and Mary Wilkins. Anticipating most of these by a generation, he was the first to demonstrate how much the farm and village provided of literary interest.

Like Hawthorne and Longfellow, Whittier wrote of the distant past of New England in such poems as "Mogg Megone" and "The Bridal of Pennacook." But he went beyond the other two authors in writing of the everyday life of the country people, beginning long before the Civil War and continuing, even during his abolitionist activities, to the end of his life. In an essay on Robert D. Dinsmore, an obscure Scottish dialect poet long resident in New Hampshire, Whittier sets down the qualifications for the author who would write successfully of the New England countryside. He immediately excludes "the mere dilettante and amateur ruralist." Only the person brought up in and actively living in the country should attempt to write of it. Simplicity and directness of expression are indispensable—"no euphemism, or transcendentalism,—the plainer and commoner the better."[1] Dinsmore was effective because "never having seen a nightingale, he makes no attempt to describe the fowl; but he has seen the nighthawk, at sunset cutting the air above him, and he tells of it. Side by side with his waving cornfield and orchard blooms, we have the barnyard and the pigsty" (468-69).

Those who remember Whittier solely for such idyls as "Telling the Bees" and "Snowbound" may question whether Whittier followed his own recommendations of displaying the pigsty as well as the apple blossoms. Yet even "Snowbound" contains the portrait of the religious fanatic, Harriet Livermore, who wanders alone through the Holy Land in the expectation of witnessing the second coming of Christ—a character eccentric and willful enough to delight Mary Wilkins. In other poems Whittier has described in detail the sordid aspects of existence in the New England uplands. In the Prelude to "Among the Hills," after evoking the sleepy beauty of the summer landscape and commenting on the strength and dignity that such solitude sometimes imparts to those to live in it, he admits that he knows

> Too well the picture has another side,—
> How wearily the grind of toil goes on
> Where love is wanting, how the eye and ear
> And heart are starved amidst the plenitude
> Of nature, and how hard and colorless
> Is life without an atmosphere. I look
> Across the lapse of half a century,
> And call to mind old homesteads, where no flower
> Told that spring had come, but evil weeds. . . .
> And, in sad keeping with all things about them,
> Shrill, querulous women, sour and sullen men,
> Untidy, loveless, old before their time,
> With scarce a human interest save their own
> Monotonous round of small economies
> Or the poor scandal of the neighborhood. . . .
> Church-goers, fearful of the unseen Powers,
> But grumbling over pulpit-tax and pew-rent,
> Saving, as shrewd economists, their souls
> And winter pork with the least possible outlay
> Of salt and sanctity. . . .[2]

This depressing vignette of the back country, where the human stock as well as the fields and pastures have gone to seed, must be present in any gallery that purports to be representative of rural New England in the last century, and even to the present time. Whittier was too honest to exclude the unpleasant, and so was Mary Wilkins, whose art is in total accord with Whittier's theory and practice. In fact, in the kind of honesty that insists on giving a complete view of things, Miss Wilkins surpasses all other New England writers of her century, including Whittier.

II *Cult of the Peasant*

The refusal to varnish the truth was part of the credo of those New Englanders who took their writing seriously, as did most of those who wrote of the countryside. In the broadest sense these recorders of the New England decline, as Fred Pattee called them, were reflecting a world-wide literary fashion of writing about the common people, especially the peasant. George Sand in her Preface to *Légendes Rustiques* referred to the peasant as the key to the cultural origins of civilization: "the sole historian remaining to us from prehistoric times." Before George Sand, Sir Walter Scott in portrayals of the magnificent peasants Jeanie and Effie Deans in *The Heart of Midlothian* and of course the romantic poets like Burns and Wordsworth had presented the farmers and villagers of the British Isles as the fountainheads of most of the enduring values in human life. George Eliot continued the sympathetic and probing examination of peasant life, notably in *Adam Bede*. In the meanwhile, Turgenev in Russia had produced in *A Sportsman's Sketches* a compassionate record of *moujik* life; and a little later, in the work of Tolstoy and Dostoyevsky, the *moujik* became the center of what was almost a cult.

All these authors and others of Europe were being read and acclaimed in America. For instance, when several of Björnson's novels of the lives of Norwegian farmers and fishermen first were translated into English, a reviewer in the *Atlantic Monthly* in 1870 exhorted American writers to profit from the Scandinavian example and turn to their own countryside and seacoast for equally rewarding material. It was time for Americans to cease the imitation of British society novels—for example, the "blond romances" of Mrs. Muhlbach—and to draw inspiration from those Continentals who wrote of things and people of significance. Such exhortations were not in vain. Under the example and critical leadership of William Dean Howells, literary America was becoming more oriented to the Continent than to England. Indeed, John De Forest had already produced a novel or so in which the influence of French "realistic" writers like Balzac was as noticeable as that of Dickens or Thackeray.

III *Moral Earnestness*

In a national rather than a world-wide perspective, the New England regionalists like Sarah Orne Jewett and Mary Wilkins were notable contributors to the rise of an American literature indigenous in authorship, theme, and subject matter. Throughout the nineteenth century, critics had been clamoring for authors who would write about American subjects as Americans and not as imitators of the English or other Europeans. It was time, they said, to cease rehashing old-world themes. The call was for honesty as much as for originality. The exhortation was given its most eloquent utterance in Emerson's "The American Scholar" (1837), in which the commonplace daily lives of the people on the farms and in the shops were recommended to the poet or scholar as the first objects of study. Emerson relegated the great works of the past to a secondary position as sources of inspiration for independent study rather than as objects for abject imitation. The moral earnestness of Emerson's pleas appealed to most Americans, but especially to New Englanders. The sense of duty that Emerson aroused in those who wrote could not but strike a chord in minds only partially—and that quite recently—liberated from Puritanism.

Many a lesser figure echoed Emerson's appeal as the decades passed. Typical among them was Thomas Wentworth Higginson, colonel of a Negro regiment in the Civil War, minister, editor, author, and sponsor of would-be authors including Emily Dickinson. In an essay entitled "Americanism in Literature" Higginson voices the usual disapproval of American slavishness before British letters: "The Englishman is undoubtedly a wholesome figure in the mental eye; but will not 20,000,000 copies of him do for the present?"[3] He suggests that writers explore other cultures, but he is more insistent that they explore our own national character and infuse it into their writing. Good New Englander that he is, he feels that the building of a strong national literature would be aided by Puritan seriousness of purpose—a purpose he found signally lacking among the educated classes of Americans. A lyceum lecturer who knew the hinterland—Miss Wilkins had heard him in Brattleboro in 1870—Higginson found a greater boldness of thought among the rural rather than among the urban population of the United States. The country people had not become so supine before the transatlantic influences; they retained a remnant of the independence that their ancestors had voyaged four thousand miles to find and had fought several wars to secure.

Earnestness of purpose, then, was the watchword for the New England rural writers. The idea was intrinsic in Whittier's essay on Robert Dinsmore and in all his poetry. It sparked Harriet Beecher Stowe's energies in her New England books, as she states in regard to *Oldtown Folks*: "It was more to me than a story; it is my résumé of the whole spirit and body of New England, a country [*sic*] that is now exerting such an influence on the civilized world that to know it becomes an object."[4] To Sarah Orne Jewett, similarly, it became a sacred duty to make her region known to the rest of the nation because by so doing she promoted mutual understanding and unity, and she quoted Plato to prove her point. Miss Jewett believed with George Sand that, in revealing the ways of country life, she would remind her fellow countrymen of the most precious values in their tradition. Mary Wilkins, who had read both Sarah Orne Jewett and Harriet Beecher Stowe, possessed a similarly highly developed sense of purpose, which is stated in the prefaces to *A Humble Romance* and to *Pembroke*. Years later in June, 1913, in an article in *Harper's Bazar*, entitled "The Girl Who Wants to Write," she insists on an author's writing "above all things the truth" (272).

In harmony with this high sense of purpose and devotion to truth was a preoccupation with morals and conduct, what Howells named "ethicism." The spirit of the times, in fact, demanded a focus upon ethics. Matthew Arnold had estimated conduct to be "three fourths of life." Tolstoy, who was being promoted in the United States by Howells, had concluded that literature without moral purpose could not justify its existence and had taken to writing his famous parables, which Mary Wilkins and other New Englanders read and admired. Elizabeth Phelps Ward, author of the incredibly popular *Gates Ajar*, stated the case for "ethicism" forcefully and succinctly in her autobiography in a chapter significantly headed "Art for Truth's Sake": "In a word, the province of the artist is to portray life as it is; and life *is* moral responsibility."[5] The viewpoint is not so unesthetic as it sounds, for Mrs. Phelps realizes that a work of art must convey its lesson intrinsically: " 'Helplessly to point the moral' is the least thing needful or artistic. The moral takes care of itself. Life is moral struggle. Portray the struggle and you need write no tract."[6]

One need read very few pages of Mary Wilkins to realize that to her also life is moral struggle—the struggle within the soul of two wills opposing each other, one driving the individual on to destruction, the other to salvation. No wonder that Henry James, a giant among American moralists, was reported to be reading Miss Wilkins' stories with "enormous enthusiasm."[7] There is not a story from her pen that does not analyze human motives with the view of exposing which ones lead to misery and which to happiness. And this is just what James has done in such novels as *The Portrait of a Lady* and *Daisy Miller*, in both of which excessive independence—the equivalent of excessive willfulness in Miss Wilkins' stories—brings havoc to the heroines and those associated with them. Both Daisy Miller and Isabel Archer attempt to prove themselves right before a world which considers them wrong. This is analogous to the drive of Miss Wilkins' Puritans to prove that one's own will, however eccentric, is God's will and therefore must be pursued regardless of social pressures. Some of James's characters, like Miss Wilkins', experience something analogous to conversion when the will shifts from a course of disaster to one of redemption. But such shifts in the characters both authors created are most difficult and sometimes impossible. Daisy Miller, like Louisa Ellis, never does achieve it. Isabel Archer, like Barnabas Thayer, does; but only after a night-long ordeal of self-examination and self-recognition, a process strongly suggestive of Jane Field's vigil and Barnabas' soul searchings.

The term "local color," therefore, is inappropriate in describing Mary Wilkins' work, though she has been repeatedly pigeonholed under that label. Local manners, speech, scenery are only a part—though an important part—of her work. "Realism," as it is defined by James in "The Art of Fiction" or by Howells in *Criticism and Fiction*, is more appropriate, but Miss Wilkins had no notion that she was a "realist" until reviewers informed her of the fact. The term "regionalist" remains perhaps the most useful to apply to Mary Wilkins, for it includes local color and realistic evocation of a place and its people without excluding the idealism and the ethical didacticism that was part of the spirit of New England in her lifetime and which she shared in a generous degree.

CHAPTER 7

God's Paupers and Man's: Two Studies in Poverty

I Jerome, A Poor Man: *Plot and Setting*

MISS WILKINS' next novel after *Madelon* marks a shift from a primary interest in the conscience and the will to a concern with the psychological effects of poverty, the chief social and economic problem in the New England of her day. The shift in interest is indicated in the subtitle of the book, *Jerome, a Poor Man*, published by Harper and Brothers in 1897. Her longest novel to date—over five hundred pages—it was not, though an improvement on *Madelon*, her best in technique or style. Among its drawbacks is its length—the result of an inordinately protracted pair of love complications, the untangling of which requires half the book. In addition, the plot depends upon several gimmicks that stretch the reader's powers of belief beyond the breaking point.

The action is set in motion by the disappearance, interpreted as suicide, of the twelve-year-old Jerome's father, who had been fighting a losing battle against a poverty that would become total destitution upon the imminent foreclosure of the mortgage on his farm. Despite the absence of a corpse, a funeral is held; and then his family sets about the task of survival without him. At the end, however, Abel Edwards, the father, reappears, a broken old man. All the time, he divulges, he had been working on a farm twenty miles away, amassing the money to pay the mortgage. Very likely Miss Wilkins had in mind Hawthorne's "Wakefield," the story of a man who on a whim vanishes from his wife in London by merely moving into the next street but returns to her, again on a whim, after a lapse of twenty years. But the Vermont countryside, where every community is connected with every other by a network of friends and kin, is not so favorable as London for this kind of anonymity.

Another gimmick upon which the plot hinges is an agreement signed by Jerome and two grasping money-lenders in the town, Simon Basset and Dr. Prescott, to the effect that if the poverty-stricken Jerome ever received $25,000 and distributed the sum among the poor, the other two would distribute in a like manner one quarter of their fortunes. The agreement was entered into by the two wealthy men insincerely as the result of a dare growing out of a discussion in a general store. Yet it leads, rather incredibly, to the unsnarling of the seemingly hopeless tangle of relationships that the main characters get themselves into.

These absurdities are somewhat offset by the very impressive strengths of the book. The village of Upham, in which the novel is laid, is the most completely described of Miss Wilkins' fictional communities. Though at the time of writing she had been back in Randolph ten years, Upham is clearly a Vermont village. Indeed, some of the landmarks of the Brattleboro vicinity appear in it; and one of the most melodramatic events in the novel, the flooding of Graystone Brook, which destroys Jerome's sawmill, recalls the destructive flooding of Whitestone Brook in Brattleboro, an event Miss Wilkins had witnessed as a girl. But Upham suggests Vermont of the 1880's and 1890's in more basic ways. The fearful poverty among all but a handful of gentry was the condition in most hill towns, and in Upham poverty is the outstanding fact of existence and the source of the action in the novel.

Miss Wilkins shows all levels and gradations of this poverty, beginning with an appalling view of the poorhouse with its luckless population of idiots, paupers, orphans, crones, and persons only temporarily "on the town." The poorhouse is symbolically situated close to the village, for most of the townspeople are never far from destitution. Outside the poorhouse by dint of desperate and ceaseless struggle are the majority of the citizens, represented by the Edwardses and the Uphams, who cultivate pitiably small and sterile farms burdened by mortgages always on the verge of being foreclosed; by the Judds and the Lambs, who eke out a living by sewing shoes for a local entrepreneur; and by several shopkeepers not notably more prosperous than their customers. The comparative well-being of the gentlefolk and professional men, such as Lawyer Means, Dr. Prescott, Squire Merritt, and Colonel Lamson, serves only to accentuate the misery of the others.

II *The Pride of the Poor*

The bitterness of rural poverty was the subject of other writers in Miss Wilkins' day, for example, of Edgar Watson Howe and Hamlin Garland. Her originality lies in her analysis of the psychological effects of pauperism. Whether from experienced adversity in her childhood or from sympathetic yet objective observation, she commanded a depth of insight regarding poverty that was unparalleled in America in her time. Poverty, she perceived, constitutes a humiliation, especially in communities with a heritage of Calvinism, which tended to regard one's worldly state as an indication of one's standing with God. Humiliation, she further understood, has the effect of enhancing pride. And pride, if sharpened sufficiently, will express itself in acts of masochism or sadism. Elsewhere in Miss Wilkins' work—"A Village Singer" or "A Solitary"—similar consequences of humiliation from causes other than poverty had been analyzed.

As Gide has pointed out, Dostoyevsky's treatment of poverty is one phase of his treatment of humiliation in general: poor people are inordinately proud, and their pride has been enhanced by their misfortunes; the enhanced pride expresses itself in irrational acts of harm to oneself or others. Miss Wilkins had made the same observations long before she read *Crime and Punishment*, which in the characterization of Marmeladov provides an excellent example of Dostoyevsky's views on the effects of poverty. The Russian novel, however, undoubtedly confirmed Miss Wilkins in her own thinking.

A comparison of a scene dealing with poverty from Dostoyevsky's *The Brothers Karamazov*, which Miss Wilkins had not read at this time if she ever read it at all, with a like scene from *Jerome* throws light on the American's method and viewpoint. In *The Brothers Karamazov*, Captain Snegiryov—whose family consists of a son dying of tuberculosis, a crippled and mentally deranged wife, a hunchbacked daughter with withered legs, and another daughter, who is physically and mentally normal but unable, because of lack of money, to return to the university where she had been studying—has been dismissed from the army because of drunkenness and is now out of work. The family lives in "a regular peasant's room" in the direst destitution. Into their midst comes Alyosha Karamazov, bringing a present of two hundred roubles from the fiancée of Dmitri, Alyosha's brother, who in a drunken rage had dragged the Captain through the streets by his beard. Alyosha is greeted by the haughty stares of the mother, the arrogant insults of the college girl, and the mock courtesies of the Captain. Later in the open air, Alyosha offers the money to the Captain, urging him to accept "unless all men are to be enemies on earth! But there are brothers even on earth. . . . You have a generous heart, . . . you must see that, you must."[1] Alyosha understands that sometimes it requires more generosity to accept a gift than to bestow one.

At first the Captain eagerly accepts the banknotes and enumerates the benefits that will accrue from them: medicine for his sick wife and children, the return of his student daughter to the university, a new start for himself in some other town. Then suddenly he hurls the notes on the ground and "with wild fury" begins "trampling them under his heel, gasping and exclaiming . . . : 'So much for your money! So much for your money! Tell those who sent you that [I do] not sell [my] honor. . . . What should I say to my boy if I took money from you for our shame?"[2] Thus he refuses to accept, though his son is doomed to die unless a way is found to pay for doctors. Later, Alyosha attempts to analyze the Captain's perversity. He is "one of those awfully sensitive poor people."[3] He has been injured and insulted, or at least feels he has been, and it is difficult for others to approach such people as benefactors. All the time the Captain had had the presentiment that he would reject the money, but he had masochistically allowed himself to become ecstatic over the gift so that the ultimate refusal of it would hurt the more.

In *Jerome*, Adoniram Judd's family, kin to the Edwardses, lives with one foot in the poorhouse. The Judd dwelling is mortgaged, the son is blind, work is scarce. The son's blindness can be cured, if money can be found to send him to Boston for an operation. Jerome, who has been saving to buy a sawmill, offers the money, but Mrs. Judd, like Captain Snegiryov, refuses. To accept the money, she asserts, would be worse than letting her son remain blind: "Nobody shall sacrifice himself for my son. If our own prayers and sacrifices are not sufficient, it is the will of the Lord that he should suffer, and he will suffer" (406). More important than her son's eyesight to Mrs. Judd is her honor, her determination to "be beholden to no one." She has been injured by Providence, by the Lord, just as Captain Snegiryov has been injured by Dmitri; and injury, whether human or divine in origin, only deepens humiliation and heightens pride until resentment becomes so agonizing that it glories in pain to oneself and to one's family.

Mrs. Judd's refusal, some may think, might be in part the result of an unwillingness to take Jerome's hard-earned money. But such an explanation is undermined by her second refusal of help. When Jerome unexpectedly inherits $25,000 from Colonel Lamson, he divides the sum among the one hundred poorest people in the town in accord with the agreement he had made on a dare some years before. The Judds are thus eligible to receive $250. Moreover, Dr. Prescott, who is party to the agreement, decides to write off a number of mortgages, one of them on the Judd homestead. Mrs. Judd's refusal of both offers is notable for its emotion rather than its logic: "I shan't take money that's given in any such way, and neither will my son. . . . We shan't take what Dr. Prescott has offered neither—to give us the mortgage on our house. It's an honest debt, and we don't want to shirk it. If we're paupers, we'll be paupers of God, but of no man!" (482).

A similar pride is the foundation of Jerome's character, which is one of the most convincingly and sympathetically delineated in all of Miss Wilkins' works. In the opening pages of the book, Jerome, aged twelve, betrays his pride when he refuses to accept some gingerbread from the Squire's daughter, Lucina, who will one day be his bride. But having rudely refused her gift, he insists on giving Lucina a piece of sassafras root that he has dug in a swamp; and she, not being poor, has the grace to accept it. He comes by his pride in his home; in the early pages his mother, a hopeless cripple, insists on sending to wealthy Mrs. Prescott her "china bowl with pink flowers on it" (14) full of parsnip soup in return for a pitcher of lamb broth that Mrs. Prescott had sent her. Though Mrs. Judd's children go hungry that evening, she has the satisfaction of saying: "Now I guess Mis' Doctor Prescott won't think we're starvin' to death here, if her husband has got a mortgage on our house" (17).

III *Pride of Spirit*

All through his life Jerome is generous to a fault. As a boy, he gives his time and strength to his family, of which he is the sole support after the disappearance of his father. Later he learns something of medicine, the use of herbs and the diagnosis and treatment of the more common diseases, so that he can treat free of charge those who are too poor to pay Dr. Prescott's exorbitant fees. Working furiously to buy a sawmill so that he can earn enough to marry Lucina, he freely offers his savings to any one in need, like the Judds and his Uncle Ozias Lamb; and later, he apportions his unexpected inheritance among the village poor. Though the religious revivals that occasionally excited the town never brought him to conversion, he is convinced of God's justice and that his own duty is "to apply his small strength towards furthering what he could, if no more than an atom, of the eternal will . . ." (262). Clearly God's will is to help the poor, so Jerome throws himself into the task. Calvinistically, when things go wrong and he loses his mill in a flood, he regards his misfortune as "the whip-lash for sin" (454) that he might have committed. And when, on receiving his inheritance, he is tempted to keep it for himself, contrary to his signed pledge, he ransacks his conscience with a skill that would do credit to the Mathers and which Miss Wilkins attributes to his "generations of Calvinistic ancestors" (465). In the end, Jerome stands by his promise and his purpose, which he identifies with the will of God.

Jerome, moreover, has his moments of mystical insight. Walking on a country road one spring dusk, he "had a vague impression which he did not express to himself, that he had come to a door wide open into spaces beyond all needs and desires of the flesh and the earthly soul, and had a sense of breathing new air. . . . The image even of the beautiful Lucina, which had dwelt with him since Sunday, faded, for she was not yet become of his spirit . . ." (282).

But despite his good works (which in Calvinism are secondary to faith) and despite his moments of insight, Jerome remains unconverted; for his generosity, however heroic, has been a manifestation of spiritual pride, the deadliest of all sins. He gives but he refuses to receive. When friends offer him help after the loss of the mill, he rejects aid as summarily as would the Judds. He will be God's pauper, not man's. Lucina, whom he loves and who is well-off in her own right, becomes physically ill because he will not ask her to marry him until he has earned enough to support her in the style of living to which she is accustomed; and he persists in this stubbornness, though he has come to acknowledge that love is "the one truth and reality and source of all things" (497). Finally, fed up with his obstinacy, Lucina's mother confronts him with the truth about himself: "You generous—you! Talk of Simon Basset! You are a miser of a false trait in your own character. You are a worse miser than he, unless you give it up. What are you, that you should say, 'I will go through life, and I will give, and not take'? What are you, that you should think yourself better than all around you—that you should be towards your fellow-creatures as a God, conferring everything, receiving nothing? If you love my daughter, prove it. Take what she has to give you, and give her, what is worth more than money, if you had the riches of Croesus, the pride of your heart." Jerome asks: "Is it pride or principle?" And she answers: "Pride" (502).

At this moment Jerome undergoes conversion, perhaps not in a form acceptable to the church deacons, but nevertheless a true change of heart. Jerome in no way associates his spiritual metamorphosis with religion, but Miss Wilkins does. The direction of a stubborn will is reversed by a supreme, counteracting effort of will. One assumes that Jerome's generosity, his compassion for the poor, will remain, but not as manifestations of pride. He is now truly one of God's elect, rather than one of God's paupers. If the change seems sudden, one must recall that conversion by definition is sudden; and New England villagers like Miss Wilkins, as well as her characters, were used to suddenness in conversions. But, in fact, Jerome's change of heart is not unexpected. It is more remarkable—a testimony to the strength of his will—that he held out so long.

IV *Style*

Though marred by a preposterous plot, *Jerome* is among Miss Wilkins' best in style. In *Madelon* she had blemished the simplicity and vividness of her early manner by attempting to complicate and vary her sentence structure. The device she depended upon for this end was inversion of word order. The effect was clumsy and artificial, especially since the inversions were accompanied by a pseudo-archaic diction: "Sorely afraid was Dorothy Fair, if the truth were told, to go with this passionate girl, who had declared to her face that she had done murder . . ." (*Madelon*, 96). In *Jerome* she has not returned entirely to the primer-like simplicity of her short stories, which was effective enough in them but slightly palling in the novels *Jane Field* and *Pembroke*.

Rather, she has achieved a style that is natural but sufficiently involved for the length and complexity of the novel form. Her sentences are varied in structure but not artificially; her diction is concrete; her paragraphs, especially the descriptive ones, are adequately and rhythmically developed. Word pictures like those of the flooding of the millstream, Jerome's old white horse pulling a sleigh or plough, the gatherings in the local store, the poorhouse and its inhabitants are beautifully done. In these and others—for example, her countless depictions of the interiors of dwellings of both the rich and the poor—is caught the very essence of village life as it was over all New England a hundred years ago but lingers now only in the most remote regions—and there so faintly as to serve no other purpose than to certify to the genuineness of Miss Wilkins' accomplishment. Lacking the dramatic force of *Pembroke*, *Jerome* must be ranked as inferior to that novel; but it is second to none of her longer works in its rendering of an atmosphere.

V The Portion of Labor

After *Jerome* Mary Wilkins' literary output continued unabated with two more novels and four volumes of short stories within the next four years, despite the fact that her energies were being depleted by other causes. In 1897, the same year that she had published *Jerome*, she had become engaged to marry Dr. Freeman of Metuchen, New Jersey. A year or so later this engagement was temporarily broken, partly because Miss Wilkins felt she was needed in the Wales family, with whom she lived in Randolph. The head of the family, John Wales, had become an alcoholic and was seriously neglecting the farm which provided the family's livelihood. During this period Mary Wilkins' sleep was disturbed by dreadful nightmares, and she had to resort to sedatives in such quantities that she became partially addicted to them. She needed now to sleep next to someone who would hear her during her dreams and arouse her from them. In her waking reveries, she sometimes pictured herself as a renegade from God's ordering of things—a rebel and an outcast.

Five of the six volumes that she wrote during this troublesome time will be discussed in a later chapter. At present it is appropriate to consider *The Portion of Labor*, though it was published in 1901. Not only is it the next really ambitious novel after *Jerome*, but it is a companion piece to that book, its primary theme being poverty, a subject that had preoccupied Miss Wilkins all her life.

In *Jerome*, the dour old shoemaker Ozias Lamb, admonishes his nephew: "Don't you forget that all you came into this world for was to try not to get out of it through lack of nourishment, and to labor for life with the sweat of your brow. You don't need much eddication for that" (206). At times Ozias would be less passive and give vent to a revolutionary tirade: "What right has one [man] with the whole loaf, while another has a crumb? What right has one man with half the land in the village, while another can hardly make shift to earn his grave?" (193). Jerome ponders these questions and becomes at times as bitter as his uncle. Poverty is the condition in which most of his fellow-townsmen suffer out their lives; poverty is the one great enemy of happiness. And there are no signs of amelioration. At the end of the book, one of the main props of precarious village livelihood is removed when the shoe factory that opens in a neighboring town brings to an end the making of shoes on consignment in the village homes. All the people can do is impotently curse "the new ideas that take the bread out of poor men's mouths to give it to the rich" (463).

Jerome is a study in rural poverty of the kind that Miss Wilkins had observed in Vermont, but more particularly in Randolph where, along with the decline of agriculture, the construction of shoe factories in nearby Brockton had destroyed the home industry system on which many of her neighbors had so long depended. Economic necessity, in fact, had driven her own family to Brattleboro and had later forced her father back into carpentry as far afield as Florida, where he met his lonely death. The Wilkinses had never been threatened with starvation, but they knew what hard times could be. In all her writing, Miss

Wilkins evinces a deep sympathy with the poor that is the natural result of her own intimacy with their condition.

VI *Mill Operatives*

In *The Portion of Labor*, which explores the plight of the poor in a sizable New England manufacturing city, Miss Wilkins' discoveries in this setting are no less depressing than those in the rural one of *Jerome*. The conditions of daily life among the mill-workers are the same hard work, periods of bare subsistence alternating with near starvation, fear, bitterness, despair. Focusing upon a respectable working family, the Brewsters, whose Yankee lineage is as pure as that of the haughtiest Boston Brahmin, Miss Wilkins depicts these conditions with painful vividness and passionate indignation. One critic has designated *The Portion of Labor* as Miss Wilkins' "most ambitious and least successful novel."[4] This opinion is simply not correct. Like much of her longer fiction, it has serious weaknesses, but it also has strengths. Most impressive among the latter is the verisimilitude with which she presents the drab, gray manufacturing town with its snow-clogged streets, its offensively garish shopping area, its clanging streetcars, and its population of Yankees, Irish, Swedes, and Slavs, all merged beneath the shadow of the monolithic mills into a uniformity that blots out racial, national, and even individual differences. Such depressing cities were, and are, realities of our civilization. An effective reproduction of their atmosphere —and Miss Wilkins has done no less—is a worthwhile literary achievement. A visitor to Lowell, Lawrence, Manchester, or Brockton today, where the old brick or stone factories, many of them deserted, stretch for miles along the rivers or canals or narrow streets, will value Miss Wilkins' accomplishment in *The Portion of Labor*.

In her depiction of the workers themselves she has been equally successful, with the one damaging exception of her heroine. All of the dozen or so mill hands who play appreciable roles in the novel come convincingly to life: stolid Andrew Brewster with his hereditary New England conscience that afflicts him cruelly when he invests and apparently loses his savings in Colorado mining stock; earthy, coarse-mouthed, highly sexed Eva Loud, who marries the equally earthy and unpredictable Jim Tenny and goes insane when he deserts her for a former sweetheart; the vacuous Sadie Peele, who opposes a strike of the workers because it will mean she cannot buy the near-seal cape she had set her heart on; the hotheaded Amos Lee, who shoots at Ellen Brewster when she is leading the strikers back to work but hits and almost kills one of the owners instead; the bluff and flirtatious Irish foreman Ed Flynn, with whom half the female operatives are in love and who finally, out of pity, marries the moronic Mamie Brady after she almost does away with herself with a dose of laudanum taken in despondency brought on by his indifference to her love for him—these and others are presented with a lifelikeness that attests to Miss Wilkins' first-hand acquaintance with mill people, as well as to her competence in characterization.

The treatment of her heroine, the beautiful, brilliant, strong-willed, and idealistic Ellen Brewster, is another matter, however. Like Mary Wilkins herself as a child, Ellen is pampered and pretty and bent on getting her own way. She has been teased as teacher's "partial" at school but is the center of a small group of staunch friends because of her brightness and beauty. In her family, which like the Wilkinses is dominated by a strong-willed mother, Ellen is the center of attention. One critic has called Ellen tiresome; and she is tiresome, in the manner of the Puritans from whom she is descended. Hers is the tiresomeness of an overdeveloped sense of duty that drives her to turn down the offer of a local rich lady to put her through Vassar and that prompts her instead to take a job in the mill to help support a lunatic aunt in the asylum. It is the tiresomeness of a hypersensitive conscience that finds its expression in interminable agonizing as to whether loyalty to class and her love for a young factory owner are compatible; in this respect, Ellen would make a fine heroine for a proletarian novel. An overdeveloped sense of duty and a sensitive conscience, combined with immovable will, are commonplace in the New England of Miss Wilkins' fiction and need not surprise the reader of the novel.

But these characteristics tend to make Ellen a virago rather than the flower of femininity that Miss Wilkins would have the reader believe she is. This tendency is clear on the day of her graduation from high school when, as valedictorian, she delivers a fiery, revolutionary tirade against capitalism. The sweetness of her face prevents most of her audience from taking her seriously. But her words have their origin in a fierce pride of family and in a fanatical idealism. Her moments of religious insight, when she can stand outside herself and say to her soul, "This I will always remember," are moving in themselves and are evidence of Miss Wilkins' growing mysticism. But they do little to endear Ellen to the reader or to make her credible. Near the end of the book, she becomes a grotesque as she leads the workers back to the mill, defying the clubs, stones, and bullets of the opposing faction.

VII *Calvinistic Economics*

Miss Wilkins' presentation of the factory owners and their families is also feeble. She herself came from a working-class, though not mill-working, family. Her sympathies were with the workers, and her understanding of them was instinctive and profound. But the wealthy people in *The Portion of Labor* are not only unfeeling but wooden in characterization. Miss Wilkins tries to be fair to them, to present their point of view; but she fails to interest the reader in their problems. Despairing, perhaps, of understanding them herself, she constantly emphasizes the impossibility of bridging the gap between the classes. Neither side in the industrial struggle, she reiterates, has the ability or the desire to understand the other's position.

At a time when writers like Howells, Henry George, and Edward Bellamy were flooding the book market with blueprints for social reform, Miss Wilkins had not one suggestion in regard to the betterment of the system. Whether this is a mark of realism or of political and economic ignorance is debatable. Certainly she was not callous to the suffering and wrongs inflicted upon the poor, for no one has described them more feelingly. And equally certainly she envisaged no means for their eradication. Her book is, in fact, infused with a Calvinistic fatalism that would be enraging to a reformer. She does not blame the poor for their plight, for she bypasses in this book the Calvinist notion that the poor are suffering in payment for their own or Adam's sin. But she accepts their lot as inevitable, as part of God's way with the world. The portion of labor is not what Howells or Bellamy would have it be—a fair share of what it produces. Rather, it is what the author of Ecclesiastes designates it to be: "I withheld not my heart from any joy, for my heart rejoiced in all my labor, and that was my portion of labor."

That Miss Wilkins could solve, with apparent satisfaction to herself, the problems of labor by one rather cryptic Biblical quotation is a measure of the religious orientation of her thinking. But her resort to the Scriptural words is not blind. They are uttered at the end of 563 pages of as Naturalistic a description of the evils of unemployment, low wages, capitalistic exploitation as the most convinced Socialist could desire. And they are uttered by a man, Andrew Brewster, whose pride of self and family has been bruised every month of every year of a long life, who has more than once been reduced to whimpering tears by the brutality of the industrial system, who has seen his daughter sacrifice her education, his wife take in sewing at coolie wages, his coal scuttle stand empty by a frigid stove, while he has begged for jobs shoveling snow to earn the price of a loaf of bread. There is nothing sentimental or glossing in Miss Wilkins' presentation of the lives of the poor. Yet Andrew Brewster, whose existence has been an unabating ordeal of underpaid toil and despairing unemployment, finds his answers in Ecclesiastes: "He seemed to see that labor is not alone for itself, not for what it accomplishes of the tasks of the world, not for its equivalent in silver and gold, not even for the end of human happiness and love, but for the growth in character of the laborer" (563).

To most readers Andrew's answer is ludicrously inadequate. It relates to the New England of John Winthrop and the Mathers: God has ordained that man's life on earth be hard, that he earn his bread by the sweat of his brow, that life is a proving ground for the next world. Some such realization prompts the starry-eyed Ellen to call off the strike: ". . . a fancy seized her that rebellion and resistance were hopeless, that . . . yielding to the onslaughts of fate [was] as inevitable as life itself, one of its conditions" (473). To Miss Wilkins, if the workers could keep their integrity, above all their self-respect, they would have won a spiritual battle, the only kind that really counted in her thinking. The Brewsters, like many working families, remain solid, self-reliant, churchgoing New Englanders. In older parlance, they prove themselves, despite their poverty, to be among the sanctified. In this world, their chief reward will be the knowledge that they were able to endure; in the next, the reasonable expectation is that the rewards will be greater if not more tangible.

VIII *Lucy Larcom*: An Idyl of Work

The orthodox Calvinistic attitude towards work is well summed up by Lucy Larcom, herself an operative in the Lowell mills in the 1840's, and later a professor of literature and a poet of some standing: ". . . we were taught to work almost as if it were a religion; to keep at work, expecting nothing else. It was our inheritance, handed down from the outcasts of Eden. And for us, as for them, there was a blessing hidden in the curse."[5] In a book-length, blank-verse poem called *An Idyl of Work* Miss Larcom attempts to square the Puritan outlook with the steadily deteriorating working conditions in New England. Insisting on the basic dignity of all labor, she rejects strikes as substituting one tyranny for another, and she finds communal schemes like that tried at Brook Farm intolerably stultifying to individual liberty. The only course for the exploited worker is to struggle on by himself, extricating himself somehow from the position of the exploited,

> for nobody should moil
> Just to add wealth to men already rich.
> Only a drudge will toil on, with no hope
> Widening from well-paid labor.[6]

Both Lucy Larcom and Mary Wilkins, then, reduce the worker's problem to a spiritual one to be met and solved by the worker himself within his soul. In other words, these two writers approach the matter religiously, Calvinistically.

Whatever can be said against the Calvinist point of view, it is not sentimental or mawkish. It in no way, in any area, attempts to slur over evil or to argue that good must come of evil, as some less robust branches of Protestantism have argued. God has given men a hard world to live in. If he survives its hardship with a pure soul, he may enjoy a better one. The ruthlessness of business in oppressing the laborer is deplorable, but it is probably simply a part of God's dispensation. This view does not differ essentially from that of the scientific determinists who were already rising on the literary and philosophical scene as Miss Wilkins was writing. Dreiser in *The Financier* or in *The Titan* and

Frank Norris in *The Pit* present the brutality of big business as a manifestation of the natural law of the survival of the fittest. Those whom the Cowperwoods and Jadwins crush are perhaps pitiable, but their extinction at the hands of stronger men is inevitable. Only by thus permitting the strong to dominate the weak does nature insure the evolutionary improvement of the species. Neither Norris nor the early Dreiser sees any hope for the men-ciphers upon whom the strong necessarily prey. They are victims of the eternal order of things.

To the Calvinist, the suffering of the poor is God's ordering of things; to the naturalist, it is nature's ordering. But writers like Lucy Larcom and Mary Wilkins part company with the naturalists by setting off an area, restricted though it may be, where the irrevocable scheme slightly favors the victims. Rather than dehumanizing them into ciphers, these Calvinist writers give them a chance to battle for their humanity—for their selfhood and integrity. Grim though Calvinistic determinism may be, it is less harsh than that of social Darwinism or of dialectical materialism.

CHAPTER 8

Excursions into the Past and Other Diversions

IN THE DECADE between publication of *A New England Nun* (1891) and *The Portion of Labor* (1901), Miss Wilkins' major effort went into the five novels thus far discussed. She had become thoroughly professional, had no trouble finding a market for her product, and enjoyed an almost uniformly favorable press both in America and in England. The energies of this New England spinster were seemingly limitless; in addition to the five big novels, she published during this decade two lesser novels, a play, and four volumes of short stories. For an author whose frequently avowed purpose was to record qualities of New England's past in the New England of her day, it is not surprising that three of these books—the play, one collection of short stories, and one novel—record excursions into history.

I *Salem as Archetype*

Through both her mother's family and her father's, Miss Wilkins could trace her ancestry to the earliest settlement of Salem. Most colorful among these forebears was Bray Wilkins, who with the help of six stout sons and an indomitable will cleared and cultivated hundreds of acres of Essex County land and established his family as one of the most prosperous and prolific in eastern Massachusetts. Late in life Bray Wilkins had had a part in getting his grandson hanged as "a witch," from spite probably more than from a conviction that the young man had sold his soul to Satan. The consciences of New Englanders had been smarting under the stigma of the Salem witchcraft delusion ever since Judge Sewall had stood before the congregation of his church while the minister read his confession of guilt as one of the judges at the witch trials. As any one who has read Hawthorne knows, the pangs of conscience had not been deadened even as late as the mid-nineteenth century. Hawthorne's ancestor, of course, John Hathorne, had been one of the magistrates arraigning the suspects, and Hawthorne wondered how many generations the taint would continue to cloud the current of his family's history. Beyond question, Mary Wilkins had read the introduction to *The House of the Seven Gables*, where Hawthorne states his misgivings, and she too must have thought of the part her ancestors had had in that dark drama. For both as witnesses and accusers they had been deeply involved, but not so prominently as John Hathorne.

Unlike Hawthorne, Miss Wilkins took upon herself no burden of guilt for the mistakes of her ancestors, but her interest in Salem is clearly more than that of the objective historian. In 1892, exactly two hundred years after the Salem delusion reached its climax, Mary Wilkins published in the December issue of *Harper's New Monthly* a six-act tragedy, *Giles Corey, Yeoman*, the title character of which had the distinction of being executed by pressing—by being crushed under a weight rather than being hanged. The play gives proof that Miss Wilkins had a thorough knowledge of the Salem trials and those involved in them. Much on the subject had been published in the nineteenth century, including the complete records of the evidence presented in court. But her characterization of Giles Corey himself and his wife Martha, also executed as a witch, indicates beyond question a close acquaintance with, and perhaps a sole reliance on, Charles W. Upham's famous two-volume *Salem Witchcraft* published in 1866 and today a respected authority on its subject. Upham's approach was methodical in the extreme; indeed, his book may have had a far-reaching influence on all of Miss Wilkins' writing about New England since he presents in it an archetypical New England village. Before recounting the events of the delusion, he gives a three hundred-page history of Salem from its founding in 1628 to the beginning of the trials in 1691, as he believed that only against such a background could later events be understandable. One can imagine Miss Wilkins' feelings as she read these preliminary pages.

Life in Salem, as Upham describes it, was as much a function of the Calvinistic will and conscience as life in the Vermont and Massachusetts villages is in Miss Wilkins' fiction. Salem had been established by faith and will power pitted against a rocky land, a harsh climate, and hostile aborigines. But within the lifetime of Bray Wilkins, who lived to be ninety-two, the old energies had begun to be diverted into channels destructive to the individual and society alike. The villagers' lives were tyrannized by gossip, by what people might think, as in Miss Wilkins' stories. Neighbor was turned against neighbor in jealousy or in long-nurtured, long-dormant grudges. Though Indians still threatened from the nearby forests, Salem became preoccupied with its own ingrown, isolated self. The latent animosities of fifty years erupted into an orgy of mutual extermination involving the entire populace, from girls of ten or twelve to grandsires in their eighties. So slight a cause as a wrangle over a minister's wood supply might release hates that terminated in executions.

II *"There be that which is beyond human ties to force a man"*

Upham gives much attention to Giles, whom he regards with unstinted admiration. His story is simple in outline, but very human and very inspiring in its outcome. Corey was a prosperous farmer and the father of four married daughters, all by the first of his three wives. But during his long life he was often the focal point of scandal and gossip. Strong, bold, and rough, he had been accused of murdering his hired man. The fact was that he had severely beaten the man for loafing, and the man had died later in Corey's house while Mrs. Corey was nursing him. In court, murder was not proved, and Corey was let off with a fine. On another occasion he was accused of maliciously setting fire to the house of John Proctor, who was later himself a victim of the witch-hunting. This time Giles was fully acquitted of the charges and successfully sued his accusers for defamation. Yet there can be little question that there had been irregularities in Giles's life, however exaggerated by village gossip. He was litigious, quick to use his fists, a drinker, and—worst of all—cared little for "what folks will think."

Then astonishingly, at the age of eighty, he got religion and confessed his sins. He convinced the minister and the deacons of the genuineness of his change of heart and was admitted as a full church member and communicant. He had become one of the saints of the church. But with conversion came trouble, for this was the time that the "afflicted girls" first attracted public and official notice and began making their reckless charges. At first Giles enthusiastically attended the judicial hearings and with all the zeal of a new convert supported the clergy in their search for witches. But his extremely devout third wife, Martha, who spent all her spare moments in prayer and was a model of piety, vigorously and outspokenly denied that there were any witches in Salem, announced that she would personally open the magistrates' eyes to their error, and criticized Giles's interest in the proceedings. Giles, who had the setness of many of Miss Wilkins' fictional characters, was not one to submit to female dictation. Thoughtlessly he made remarks that were later used against Martha: she had prevented him from praying; she had unsaddled the horse he was going to ride to the hearings; an ox and a cat of his had taken sick under circumstances suggestive of diabolic influence.

At length Martha was arraigned and examined before John Hathorne and Jonathan Corwin, with the Reverend Mr. Samuel Parris taking the minutes, which are printed in full in Upham's work. The authorities also drew up a deposition in which Giles Corey accused his wife of suspicious actions, but it was not sworn to before the magistrates. Giles apparently already repented his loose talk and balked at making a legally attested statement. Two of his sons-in-law were more cooperative, however, providing evidence not only against his wife but against Giles himself. His refusal to give testimony, of course, angered the officials; in fact, it proved to be his own death warrant. Martha was brought to trial and condemned to hang; the following Sunday the church excommunicated her. One of the three people in Salem unswervingly to deplore the folly of the witch persecution, she uttered upon the very gallows a prayer and a protestation of innocence that deeply impressed the spectators. Her steadfastness and piety were influential in bringing the townspeople back to sanity. She was, in fact, in the last group to be hanged. The public and the magistrates had had enough.

But perhaps more of a jolt to the public conscience was the peculiarly horrible death of Giles on September 19, 1692, just three days before Martha's martyrdom. When called into court to answer to the grand jury's indictment, he refused to plead either guilty or not guilty. By English practice at that time, if the prisoner remained "mute" after being brought before the court three times, he could be sentenced to *peine forte et dure*: be placed on his back and have successively heavier weights applied to his chest until he consented to plead or died. One motive that prompted accused persons to stand mute was to thwart the confiscation of their property, which would occur if they were convicted; and Giles, it is thought, was partly actuated by this motive. Strongly incensed against the two sons-in-law who had joined in the accusation against his wife and grateful to the ones who had remained loyal, he had caused a deed to be drawn up whereby he conveyed all his property to the latter. The document had been signed, sealed, delivered, and witnessed according to law while Giles was in Ipswich jail. Its legality could not be challenged unless he were convicted of witchcraft, as he most certainly would be if brought to trial. If Giles remained firm in refusing to plead before the court, his property would be disposed of as he wished. The deserving would be rewarded and the undeserving punished. All depended on Giles's will power, which proved equal to the challenge.

This motive by itself would be an acceptable one, but Upham speculates that Giles had other purposes in standing mute. On the basis of what is known of Giles's character, especially his profession of religion so late in life, Upham assumes that Giles was a man of conscience as well as iron will. Disgusted with himself for succumbing to the public hysteria and being somewhat to blame for Martha's conviction, Giles, Upham believes, suffered "great distress of mind" while in prison.[1] He wished not only to safeguard his property but "to expiate his own folly by a fate that would satisfy the demands of the sternest criticism on his conduct [and] proclaim his abhorrence of the prosecutions. . . . He knew that the gates of justice were closed, and that truth had fled from the scene. He would have no part nor lot in the matter; refused to recognize the court, made no response to its questions, and was dumb in its presence. He stands alone in the resolute defiance of his attitude. He knew the penalty of suffering and agony he would have to pay; but he freely and fearlessly encountered it. All that was needed to carry his point was an unconquerable firmness and he had it."[2] Giles was pressed to death beneath a weight of stones in a field near Salem jail and so "bore his testimony against the wickedness and folly of the times in tones that reached the whole world, and will resound through all the ages."[3]

The story of this farmer and his wife who could muster a will for the right which elevated them to the ranks of the martyrs could not but appeal to Miss Wilkins. Especially would Giles, whose name stands as the title of the play, impress her. His late conversion, his foolish and stubborn initial zeal for the witch hunting, his later revulsion (a sort of second conversion) when he sees the harm that he has done, and his ensuing unwavering perseverance in his new and better course—these steps in his development parallel the actions of many of her stories. Whether the Upham interpretation of Giles's motives is correct or not, it was as if ready made for Miss Wilkins, who availed herself freely of it. In her play Giles, as he is about to submit to his ordeal, gives this answer to his daughter who has been urging him to give in: "There be that which is beyond human ties to force a man, there be that which is at the root of things."[4] He speaks like one who has found God's will to be working within him, which is how a Calvinist convinced of his right must speak. His execution, he realizes, will shake the people into their senses; and he proclaims that "he has the power to die as he will and no man greater."[5]

In the case of Giles, of course, there were no trial records and only several very brief affidavits. Upham's speculations, though founded on the facts available, provide less reliable material for characterization than do the records he prints of Martha's hearings preliminary to her indictment. The calm, unshakable, slightly sarcastic woman of the actual proceedings is the same as in the play. Miss Wilkins has transcribed almost verbatim many of the speeches of the witnesses, the magistrates, and the accused. Especially cogent is her use of Martha's constantly reiterated statement, "I am a gospel woman," which in its simplicity sets her apart from all the others in the room who are actuated by varying degrees of hypocrisy, insincerity, or uncertainty as to their feelings.

III *The Intrusion of Sentimentality*

Miss Wilkins had all the ingredients of a powerful play. Yet she failed in her undertaking and for reasons not immediately clear. The fact that in respect to plot she deviated from the court records and historical facts does not of itself constitute a fault. Any dramatist would do so. But in at least one of her licenses she was unfortunate: superimposed on the witchcraft drama is the fictitious story of romantic love between young Olive Corey, a daughter of Martha and Giles (in reality they had no children), and a young and desirable suitor, Paul Bayley. Out of this affair stems Martha's persecution, for one of the "afflicted girls" has been jilted by Paul, and she and her mother maliciously implicate the Corey family in the hope of getting Paul back. Their attempts are unsuccessful, and Giles leaves his property to the young couple (another deviation from history) who are married the day of his pressing and who overhear his dying screams. The result is to detract from the social and spiritual import of Martha's and Giles's suffering and to reduce the drama to the level of domestic tragedy. Furthermore, Miss Wilkins' dialogue is disappointing when compared to the terse, colloquial, ironic New England speech of which she proves herself a master in her stories and novels of contemporary life. In *Giles Corey*, except where the author closely transcribes the records, the characters speak like stage bumpkins with a few added archaisms, like "an you say so" and "I trow," which incidentally the remarkably unarchaic English of the records does not justify. Also the insertion of a spinning song and a rather good-natured witches' song suggests a bucolicism that must have been singularly lacking in Salem.

Despite its moderate sentimentalization of history, *Giles Corey* is at least interesting to read. Lawrence Hutton, writing in *Harper's*, surmised that Miss Wilkins had intended it as closet drama, and as such he considered it mildly successful. It was presented on the stage in the spring of 1893 in Boston and New York without much success. Miss Wilkins' only serious attempt at drama, its chief interest, and an important one, in the body of her work is the evidence it gives of her thoughtful awareness of the past of New England. At the very least her reading of Upham sharpened her perception of the psychological make-up of New England villagers—their jealousies and personal animosities, their burdens of humiliated pride and their willful eccentricities, their fierce and irrational obstinacy, their agonizings of conscience, and their painful soul-searchings, as well as their triumphant moments of illumination, self-sacrifice, and love. Her study of Salem was good preparation for her writing of *Pembroke, Madelon,* and *Jerome.*

IV Silence and Other Stories

Silence and Other Stories is a volume of six short tales, all but one of which are laid in the past of New England. The title piece deals with the Deerfield Massacre of 1704. The plot, hinging on sentimental love, need not concern us. But the presentation of life in a frontier settlement, the unfailing wills and the optimism of the people in the face of frightful hardship, testify to the author's admiration for the older Puritans whose stubborn purposefulness served a worthwhile end and was not expended on petty feuds and personal crotchets as in the decaying culture of her own times. Several of the lesser characters—for example, iron-willed Widow Eunice Bishop, whose needles clash like swords as she knits—are amusingly drawn.

In another story, "The Little Maid at the Door," Miss Wilkins again draws from the history of Salem but less significantly than in *Giles Corey*. The more important historical names—the Proctors, Cotton Mather, Parris, Nancy Warren—are paraded across the pages, but the people themselves do not live, least of all the terror-stricken little Proctor girl, who has been left alone in her parents' house after their arrest.

The strongest of the stories in the volume is "A New England Prophet," which relates an incident suggested by the Millerite hysteria of the 1840's. Like William Miller, the prophet of the story has convinced himself and his followers that the world will end on a certain day. At the appointed time, the band of believers, dressed in flowing muslin robes, marches up a hill to await the end, only to march down again when the dawn arrives as usual. During the night the prophet's daughter, torn between loyalty to him and love for a young man, has yielded to the latter and been married to him.

In this story are all the ingredients of Miss Wilkins' strongest fiction: the fanatical prophet, fierce, unyielding, and humorless in his irrational conviction; the eruption of violent emotion among his following of hitherto repressed farmfolk and villagers; the reversion to sanity at the end. The prophet, like Miller himself, is one of a long line of visionaries beginning in the extreme Protestantism of Old England and including in New England such zealots as Anne Hutchinson, many leaders of the Great Awakening, Joseph Smith, and William Lloyd Garrison. No one was more aware than Miss Wilkins of the explosiveness of the

New England character, which might be manifested in some personal reprisal, as in "A Village Singer," or in a political or religious upheaval of great magnitude. In "A New England Prophet" this potential of the Yankee character for violent, tangential action is exhibited fully.

"A New England Prophet," moreover, perfectly illustrates Miss Wilkins' kinship with Hawthorne. The prophet is suggestive of dehumanized fanatics, like Hollingsworth or Ethan Brand, who pursue their ends with such undeviating volition that they destroy not only themselves but many of those unfortunate enough to cross their paths. Next to indifference, excessive zeal was to Hawthorne the darkest of sins. The zealot, whether a scientist, a reformer, or a man bent on personal revenge, violates the humanity of others and ends by turning his own heart to stone. The only antidote to such poison is the warmth of normal human affection—especially the tenderness that arises between the sexes. Thus in *The House of the Seven Gables* the pall of bigotry and greed that has darkened generations of Pyncheons is dispelled finally by the love of Phoebe and Holgrave. In "A New England Prophet" the marriage of the prophet's daughter to her very normal lover the night of the Second Coming is not just a sentimental obtrusion but marks the triumph of human goodness and common sense over headstrong, self-delusive aberration.

If this story were placed in a collection of Hawthorne's tales, one would be hard put to identify it as the work of another author. Yet Miss Wilkins conducted her analysis of the New England psyche quite independently of Hawthorne. In fact, her results are the product of intuitive rather than of methodical analysis. Thus her insights are not uniformly profound. Constantly coloring her observations with her own feelings, she frequently slips into sentimentality, especially in her later work. Her strength and her weakness both stem from her total lack of intellectuality, and here of course she differs radically from Hawthorne, whose depth of insight she achieves only sporadically.

The one story in *Silence* that is laid in the present, "Evelina's Garden" (which was also published separately in 1899) deserves mention, for it was a favorite of Miss Wilkins. It too invites comparison with Hawthorne. As in "Rappaccini's Daughter," a garden takes precedence, in a warped mind, over humanity and its happiness. Living in complete isolation from her fellow beings, Evelina, who is of a lineage superior to that of the other townspeople, devotes herself entirely to the cultivation of flowers. She has been frustrated in love, to be sure, but the frustration is the result of her family pride, which renders her incapable of letting her lover, of lower social station, know even by a glance that she returns his feelings for her. So she rejects humanity for flowers, even ceasing to attend church. In her will she demonstrates the seemingly total dehumanization of her heart by leaving to her niece, also named Evelina, her very substantial fortune under the provisos that she never marry and that she devote her life to the garden.

There has been an understanding between the local minister and the younger Evelina that they will eventually marry, but the minister now breaks the engagement from an excessive sense of duty—so excessive, in fact, that it is as dehumanizing as the elder Evelina's floral obsession. The minister, who is an embodiment of conscientious scruples rather than a man, rejects the many overtures of the girl, who is more than willing to give up her aunt's fortune. Eventually, she sprinkles the flowers with boiling brine, thereby depriving herself of her inheritance; and the minister in a burst of penitent gratitude marries her.

Up to this point Miss Wilkins has written with a firm hand a story of twofold dehumanization overcome by the wholesome and poignant emotion of young love. Unfortunately, she insists on going one step further by passing off the eccentric will as being merely a means of testing the love of Evelina for the minister, who turns out to be the beneficiary in the event that Evelina mistreats the flowers. Such mutilation of an otherwise delicately conceived story is all too common in Miss Wilkins' writing; it is additional evidence that she was guided by her heart rather than by her head.

V The Heart's Highway

Silence and Other Stories was mainly historical fiction. In 1900 Miss Wilkins again returned to the historical genre with a novel of colonial Tidewater Virginia, *The Heart's Highway*. Miss Wilkins' acquaintance with the Tidewater arose from extensive sojourns at Old Point Comfort, where she had found relief from the protracted disappointment of New England spring weather.

Her motive in writing the book, aside from cashing in on the popularity of historical fiction, has been described as the urge "to satisfy a craving for the frankly beautiful and romantic. . . ."[6] If this is the case, she cannot be accused of curbing her appetite. The beauty of the flowering days and scented nights of the May countryside caresses her pages like a benediction. The excitement of intrigue and open rebellion spurred by Nathaniel Bacon carries the reader along surely and swiftly. The story, centered on the passion between Harry Wingfield and the willful, beautiful rebel Mary Cavendish, imparts to *eros* the ultimate of glamor. The triumphant closing sentence in the book reads: "The blazon of love is the only one which holds good forever through all the wilderness of history, and the path of love is the only one which those that may come after us can safely follow unto the end of the world" (308).

The love celebrated in *The Heart's Highway* is indeed solely *eros*, unleavened by *agape*, untrammeled by religious scruples, only insignificantly impeded by social convention. The hero and heroine, of course, remain chaste while unwedded, for the novel was written in 1900. But the depiction of the Barry brothers living unmarried on their plantation with their magnificently carnal Negro mistresses who carouse with their masters and their guests (and the guests' equally carnal white wives) provides a spectacle of unrestraint remarkable from the pen of a maiden lady of nearly fifty who had hitherto confined herself, except in the case of the French and Indian Madelon, to accounts of the chilly amours of latter-day Puritans.

Most creditable to Miss Wilkins is the fact that she writes of these things, which must have seemed shocking to her contemporaries, without the least trace of salaciousness, accepting and presenting them as natural and even wholesome fulfillments of human needs. One suspects that in the imagined freedom of bygone Cavalier society Miss Wilkins was finding a relief from the frozen norm of New England morality, just as in the Virginia climate she found relief from the sleet of the New England March and April. Her main impulse, rather than to write of the beautiful and the romantic, was very likely to write of the free and uninhibited. Here was a society where even the parson could frequent the taverns and gamble and race his horses and attend the carousings of the Barry brothers and their women without being waited on by a committee of long-faced elders suggesting he submit his resignation. The fact is that the hearty Anglican parson is, in spite of his peccadilloes, an able and respected minister and a compassionate and understanding friend.

Liberation from unduly confining restraints, rather than the sovereign sway of love, is indeed the basic theme of *The Heart's Highway*. The finest scenes record an abandon entirely unrelated to love. Such are the invasions of the plantation fields by drunken mobs of commoners and aristocrats, men and women, combined in the purpose of destroying the young tobacco plants so as to cheat the king out of revenue. Led at first by the planters themselves, the mobs soon break out of control and engage in an orgy of destruction that lasts throughout the night. Though Miss Wilkins presents these riots as the first rumblings of the independence movement in the North American colonies, she is fascinated not by the political implications but by the eruption of sheer destructive human passion, free of any restraint, terrifying and thrilling at the same time, amoral rather than immoral, and capable under skillful leadership of serving useful purposes—but above all intensely, most significantly human.

Purporting to be the reminiscences of Harry Wingfield, the story successfully catches the stylistic flavor of a Defoe or a Fielding novel, along with these authors' healthy acceptance of the more passionate human emotions. In characterization the novel is strong. Harry Wingfield's excessively romantic outlook is tempered into credibility by a rather earthy practical viewpoint that he exhibits in his pithy comments on life as it unfolds about him. The heroine, Mary Cavendish, is rescued from the realm of the mawkish by her active participation in the tobacco riots. The lesser characters—the Barry brothers and their Negresses, the parson, and Mary's intense older sister, almost a Puritan in her taut self-control, supply the book with a flesh-and-blood population that does much for its readability.

Though better than most historical novels of Miss Wilkins' period, *The Heart's Highway* will doubtless never again be widely read. Such novels must be more than competent if they are to survive. This book must serve as a foil for those of her works which still live; and these are always about New England. Without knowing something about a Cavalier, one cannot fully understand a Puritan. *The Heart's Highway* aided, and was aided by, Miss Wilkins' knowledge of her native New England.

VI The Love of Parson Lord and Other Stories

Miss Wilkins' only other ventures into historical fiction were two preposterous stories in a generally very inferior collection entitled *The Love of Parson Lord and Other Stories* published in 1900. One of these, "The Tree of Knowledge," introduces cloak-and-dagger romance into the New England countryside of apparently the early nineteenth century. A well-born, hard-riding gentleman plans to hold up the Boston coach to procure money to pay his gambling debts. Foiled in this attempt by the adventitious presence of the well-born heroine at the place and time planned for the crime, he attempts to burglarize the heroine's house at night during a blizzard, is treated kindly when discovered, remains a week until the roads are passable, departs a reformed man, and returns two years later to be married. Even more ludicrous is "Catherine Carr," a story of split loyalties in Connecticut during the War of 1812.

The remaining pieces in the volume deserve some mention though they are not in the historical genre. In the title story, Parson Lord has promised God that his two daughters will be missionaries. His wife and elder daughter die, leaving him with the younger daughter, Love. The minister is now drawn between tenderness for his surviving child, whose sensitivity and whose fragile health scarcely fit her for missionary work, and his covenant with the Lord. He finds a legalistic solution to his dilemma: he refuses to marry his daughter to her lover, but he permits the local justice of the peace to do it. Thus he adheres to his agreement with God while the girl escapes the career for which he had promised her. The story is interesting mainly because it reveals the lingering of the old legalistic Covenant theology: God's and man's relations to one another are conceived as strictly contractual.

Of the two remaining stories in the volume, "Three Old Sisters and a Beau," the briefest of sketches, is a plausible account of frustrated genteel love in a New England village. The other story, "One Good Time," plays upon the theme of revolt. A mother and daughter, after the father's death, take the fifteen hundred dollars paid them as life insurance and flee to New York City from the rocky hill farm on which they have been imprisoned all their lives. Within a week they are back again, but they have had their "one good time." The daughter is now content to marry her swain of several decades and settle down to another term of imprisonment on his farm. The characterization of the girl is the best thing in the whole volume, but the story itself is seriously blemished by Miss Wilkins' descent into slapstick as she describes the adventures of the two countrywomen in the big city.

In comparison to her earlier short fiction, the whole volume marks a sad deterioration from which Miss Wilkins was only sporadically to rise. Not only has her subject matter and her treatment of it become trivial, but her style has completely lost its clipped, impressionistic quality. Conventionally long and complex sentences have replaced the short and simple structures of former volumes. The diction is less concrete and more latinized.

VII *Satire and Humor*

From the decade before Miss Wilkins' marriage in 1902 three volumes remain to be discussed. One, *Understudies*, can be dealt with better in the next chapter. The other two, humorous in nature, may be glanced at here. From 1895 to 1898 Miss Wilkins had written a series of sketches of stock village characters for the *Ladies' Home Journal*. In 1898 these were collected by the Curtis Publishing Company under the title *The People of Our Neighborhood*. It is difficult to understand why Van Wyck Brooks in *New England: Indian Summer* ranked this little volume among her three or four best. Though the book is pleasant reading, the characterization is all on the surface—a presentation of types rather than of individuals: "Timothy Sampson, the Wise Man," on whom the townspeople depend for every kind of service from doctoring their sick babies, after the physician has failed to cure them, to forecasting the weather on a day proposed for a picnic; Cyrus Emett, "the Unlucky Man," whose barns burn down as fast as he can rebuild them and whose ill luck in general is so consistent that his neighbors finally cease to try to help a man so patently unfavored by Providence; Nehemiah Stockwell, whose apple trees and potato fields yield produce when everybody else's fail and whose coddling by Providence arouses jealousy; Amanda Todd, a "friend of cats," whose frustrated love is lavished on the myriad of felines that swarm through her house and infest the environs; Phebe Ann Little, "the Neat Woman," who arises in a cold horror in the middle of the night to make sure she has swept the cellar steps, for, if they were dirty and she should die before morning, her neighbors might remember her as untidy.

These and other characters are presented with great good humor but with no attempt to get at the roots of their idiosyncrasies. The approach is that of light comedy, in contrast to that of the more seriously analytic stories of earlier collections. They convey a sense of the variety of village oddities, but give no inkling of their psychological or environmental origins. Written toward the end of the author's residence in Randolph, these sketches were modeled on her own neighbors, who tartly inquired whether Miss Wilkins thought she was so much better than her neighbors that she presumed to write about them in this manner.

In the same light vein and also written for the *Ladies' Home Journal* is the very short novel *The Jamesons*, which likewise received the praise of Van Wyck Brooks. It is one of Miss Wilkins' few attempts to exploit the conflict in a country town between "natives" and summer people. Mrs. Jameson, who comes as a boarder to Linnville, sets about improving the village in general. She reads Browning at the Sewing Circle and recommends Ibsen and Maeterlinck for the Literary Club. A health faddist, she attempts to supplant the local diet of pies and pound cake with hygienic but tasteless foods. At first resentful, the populace becomes merely amused when, having purchased a farm, Mrs. Jameson makes her chickens wear booties so that they won't scratch up the garden, mentions that she is "digging squash" and "picking potatoes," and refuses to buy a cow whose upper teeth are missing. Her love of antiques amazes them, as does her use of bean pots for vases. When her daughter, after much opposition on both sides, marries the son of a prominent village family, harmony between her and the community is finally established.

CHAPTER 9

Literary Vaudeville

ON NEW YEAR'S DAY, 1902, after many postponements during the preceding two years, Mary Wilkins and Dr. Charles M. Freeman were quietly married in Metuchen, New Jersey. The marriage turned out to be a very unhappy one, though in the early years things went smoothly enough. Dr. Freeman was eager to have his wife continue her writing, apparently viewing it as a lucrative source of income. He resented, in fact, her hours spent in cooking or other household chores because they cut into time and energy that he thought could be more profitably spent in authorship. Always prolific, Mrs. Freeman did not slacken her pace. According to one report, she simultaneously used two typewriters "on each of which was a novel."[1] She sat down to write not knowing what would come, allowing thought to suggest thought. In this manner, she could turn out seven thousand words a day. Though she wrote without planning, relying entirely on "inspiration," she revised two or three times. Most astonishing was the variety of her writing: animal stories, ghost stories, a novel written in competition with a British writer, a "cooperative novel," melodrama, not to mention a steady flow of standard fiction of all lengths. For sheer versatility she had become a master literary vaudevillist.

With a number of important exceptions, Mrs. Freeman's writing after her marriage declined in quality. One reason was of course the frantic pace at which she wrote. Though she had always written copiously, the responsibilities of a housewife were now infringing on her time. There were entertaining, a new house to build, and all the distractions of suburban living. Furthermore, Dr. Freeman was not a restful man to live with. Always a frequenter of taverns, his drinking from time to time became so excessive as to necessitate sojourns in a sanitarium. After World War I, his mind finally was affected by alcoholism, and his wife had to commit him to the New Jersey State Hospital for the Insane. Escaping in 1921, he returned home apparently much improved. But soon he began drinking prohibition liquor, and he had to be sent back to the asylum. Released once more, he lived for a time at home but later moved to his chauffeur's house. Mrs. Freeman obtained a legal separation, and Dr. Freeman drew up a will in favor of the chauffeur. When he died in 1923, Mrs. Freeman, who had been cut off with a dollar, and Dr. Freeman's four sisters, who had been left only two hundred dollars each, successfully contested the will. But by this time Mrs. Freeman, now in her seventies, had virtually ceased to write. She kept up top productivity, in fact, for only about a decade after her marriage.

As early as 1903 the deterioration in Mrs. Freeman's art had become catastrophically noticeable in a volume of ghost stories, *The Wind in the Rose-Bush and Other Tales of the Supernatural.* Deficient in suspense and atmosphere, these tales rely on the most ludicrous devices for their interest: persistently appearing shadows on a wall; items of a dead woman's wardrobe that shuttle in and out of the closet in the chamber in which she died; spectral laundry that is hung out in a vacant lot near a haunted house; a rose blossom that detaches itself from a bush and comes to rest on a dead girl's bed. With the exception of an occasional flash of Mrs. Freeman's old flair for presenting the distortion of village characters—for example, the incredible selfishness of the stepmother in the title piece—these stories are without merit.

I Six Trees

Yet in the same year as *The Wind in the Rose-Bush* appeared a volume containing some of the best writing of Mrs. Freeman's career—a collection of short stories entitled *Six Trees*, which reflects most vividly the tendency toward mysticism that had been increasingly apparent in her writing ever since *Pembroke.* "Who shall determine," she asks, "the limit at which the intimate connection and reciprocal influence of all forms of visible creation upon one another may stop? A man may cut down a tree and plant one. Who knows what effect the tree may have upon the man, to his raising or undoing?" (79-80). The answer to these questions is embodied in *Six Trees* and in another earlier collection, *Understudies* (1901): between man and the living environment are "parallels, separated perhaps by the width of the eternity of the spirit, yet as perfect and undeviating as any on the terrestrial globe" (118). The answer is, of course, completely in accord with the views of Emerson, who saw all nature as a metaphor of spirit. What one hears, sees, touches, and smells, are projections of what one thinks, intuits, or surmises. The world of the spirit and that of the senses are the two sides of the same coin. Nowhere has this Emersonian doctrine, which is the keystone of Transcendentalism, been incorporated into fiction so consciously and so successfully as in these two books.

Six Trees, especially, has won the admiration of critics; and Mrs. Freeman herself liked these stories the best of all her work. In them, she not only has full control of her craft, but she has given fullest expression to the nature mysticism that seemed to be becoming her religion. In no way was this trend irreconcilable with the modified orthodoxy of her childhood. Indeed, the concept of nature as a divine metaphor or allegory was a commonplace one among the Puritans. One finds it basic in Emily Dickinson's writings as well as in Emerson's, and it is important in Jonathan Edwards' autobiography.

A scanner of bibliographies might pass over *Six Trees* as a collection of stories held together by the gimmick of assigning to each an arboreal name. And *Understudies* might be dismissed as a double gimmick—a group of stories named after animals and a second after flowers. But these tales and sketches are more than mere literary legerdemain. Animals, flowers, and trees are as central to them as to Ovid's *Metamorphoses*. In fact, consciously or unconsciously, Mary Wilkins Freeman in these collections is carrying on the Ovid tradition. She is writing of transformations just as the Roman poet did; only hers are spiritual rather than physical. Thus in "The Lombardy Poplar" the tall slender tree, after which the story is named, typifies to an elderly spinster the self-sufficiency that she needs to break out of a lifelong subserviency to the opinions of others. Contrary to her cousin's view, she thinks the tree is beautiful; and when taken to task for expressing herself so independently, she retorts: "I'm sick of things and folks that are just like everything and everybody else. I'm sick of trees that are just trees. I like one that ain't" (148-49). The ensuing quarrel is no doubt petty and foolish, but it marks the emergence of the spinster into something like selfhood. Previously, she has been dominated by a now dead twin sister whose overbearing place in her life has been taken by the cousin. Her recognition of the individuality of the tree is the first step toward her recognition of her own. Her life has been transformed into something shapely and complete like the poplar.

Similarly in "The Elm-Tree" an old man's bitterness is transformed into tranquil acceptance when he climbs the boughs of a great elm and, harmlessly insane, finds there the shelter that a child finds in the arms of its mother. Though he has lost his reason, he is nevertheless at peace—a change not totally to be scorned. In "The White Birch," however, an equally unfortunate old man is brought by contemplation of a birch tree to a perfectly sane realization of "the dearness of that which is always left in the treasure-house of nature for those who are robbed" (64) of life's more sought-after goods. Similar transformations from discontent to peace of mind are recorded in "The Apple-Tree" and in "The Balsam Fir." The latter, a Christmas story, contains a particularly successful portraiture of a thwarted old maid who, hitherto always extremely meek, is changed into a fury and menaces with an axe a farmer who is about to cut down the fir tree near which her long-lost lover had once spoken sweet words to her. She undergoes further change the next morning, however, when she beholds the tree bedecked with snow. Her soul is now flooded with the assurance that "whatever happiness God gives He never retakes, and, moreover, that He holds ready the food for all longing, that one cannot exist without the other" (126).

These stories contain a delicate symbolism appropriate to the lives of the people involved. All are told with a sure descriptive skill and with convincing characterization. But most remarkable in the collection is "The Great Pine." A sailor, returning home after long years at sea, to the rocky hill-farm and wife and child that he had rebelliously deserted, gets lost in the wild terrain through which he is walking. Time and again he circles back to a certain lofty pine. Mrs. Freeman describes the tree in terms of the songs the wind sings among its myriad branches—songs of winter in the summer and songs of summer in the winter—for always the voice evoked in its listeners thoughts "of that which was past and to come, rather than of the present" (69). After a number of circlings back to the pine, the sailor, still a rebel, angrily sets fire to the forest—an act of spite against God. But, as with so many of Mrs. Freeman's rebellious characters, there is latent in the sailor a force that pulls him back into harmony with his lot. Following the usual sequence in Mrs. Freeman's psychology, the act of rebellion stimulates this harmonizing tendency. The sailor turns back and extinguishes the fire before it destroys the tree. For the first time he has risen "superior to his own life. . . . He, through saving the tree for himself, gained a greater spiritual growth than the tree had gained in height since it first quickened with life" (79).

No longer walking in circles, the sailor takes his way directly home to the lonely farmhouse from which he had vanished years ago. He does not find his wife, or his wife's mother, for both have died. But living in his house he finds his wife's second husband—she had thought the first one had drowned—who is half dead with consumption. There are also two children, one his own and the other the stranger's. The sailor still moves directly, not faltering in his course. With an unprecedented outburst of energy he cuts wood to sell, buys a horse, paints the house, and stocks the cellar with food. With the gentleness of Dostoyevsky's Shatov, he nurses the man who had supplanted him in his wife's bed and befriends the child of this union. Like so many of Mary Wilkins Freeman's characters in these and other stories, he has found his spiritual center. The act of saving the tree was the act of discovery. Later the tree blows down in a winter gale, but the man stands firm in spirit, transformed into something more durable than timber.

II Understudies

Animals and flowers are the subjects of the earlier book of metamorphoses, *Understudies*. The title is one of the cleverest that Mary Wilkins Freeman ever conceived. Not only are the animals and flowers members of a lower order in the organic scale—that is, they are *under* the human species—but also in many of the stories they are approximate duplications of human beings, understudies in the theatrical sense. Thus the peony in the story named for it typifies the obese woman whose favorite flower it is. The arethusa, a flower of secluded marshlands, establishes itself in the soul of a young girl who annually visits it in its lonely habitat. She identifies the retiring, beautiful blossom with the inviolable center of her own heart. Even on the day of her wedding she visits the flower, for she hopes there will always exist within her being something untouchable by even a husband. In another story, "Bouncing Bet," the flower growing in the weed-choked yard of a dilapidated mansion represents the tenacity of an elderly spinster, the last offshoot of a once-proud family, who clings to her ancestral home despite efforts of her relatives and of the selectmen to uproot her.

The flowers are symbols in the profoundest sense. They are integral parts of people's lives, part of their grasp not only of reality but, more important, of their own identities. This relationship is true even more markedly of the animal understudies. In "The Monkey," the boy and the animal are united in their mischievous, almost destructive high spirits. There is a mutual accommodation of one to the other until, in spirit and behavior, each is transformed into the other. Similarly in "The Squirrel," a farmer's sympathy for the animal whose hoard of nuts he has accidentally discovered and confiscated eventuates in his replacing the stolen supply with a bushel of walnuts bought at the local store. The way of life of both farmer and squirrel is based on conserving the growth of the summer for use in the winter. In the resemblance of means of survival the farmer senses a profounder resemblance that forces upon him, the more spiritually developed being, this act of restoration. In "The Parrot," a bird and a spinster uncannily reflect one another's feelings and moods. Not only does the bird mimic the woman's speech but gives expression to her suppressions, as when he tears the flowers from the hat of her rival who is calling with her husband, a minister whom the old maid had counted on marrying.

Most sensitive of all the animal stories are "The Cat" and "The Doctor's Horse." The former, which deals with Mrs. Freeman's favorite animal, opens with a beautiful description of the cat's hunting a rabbit in a snowstorm high up on a mountainside. Having captured his prey, the cat returns to the lonely shack, deserted in winter, where in warmer months he lives with his recluse master. After the cat's return to the cabin, an intruder breaks in. The cat gives him the rabbit, and the two share it.

All winter the arrangement continues: the cat brings game which the man cooks and scrupulously shares with him. The barrier between two kingdoms is partially breached. They live in partnership almost as equals.

In "The Doctor's Horse" the relationship between man and beast is more complex. A strong-willed doctor breaks a recalcitrant horse. But one day the horse, left in control of a timorous girl, runs away. Intractable from then on, he has to be sold. But years later, the doctor, his health shattered, unknowingly buys the same horse, which is now old and submits as formerly to his master's will. The doctor finally discovers that he is driving his former animal and with the discovery some of his youthful confidence returns. In their last years, man and beast complement each other, each adding to the other's strength and contentment.

These animal, flower, and tree stories are germane to a consideration of Mrs. Freeman as a symbolist in the tradition of Hawthorne. To begin with, they were not her first attempts in this line. In "A New England Nun" the caged canary is an unobtrusive representation of Louisa's own caged life, ruffled like the bird's feathers when threatened with masculine coarseness. "An Object of Love" deals with the relation, half affection and half resentment, between an elderly woman and her cat. Plants and animals are of course important in the quiet lives of the villagers Mrs. Freeman writes about. If one lives a lifetime in close proximity to a tree or a horse, a relationship of some depth, complexity, and significance is likely to develop, especially in the absence of the distractions of modern life. But Mrs. Freeman had for these stories many precedents, and they undoubtedly influenced her. Hawthorne's use of chickens and plants in *The House of Seven Gables* to symbolize the decadence of the Pyncheon family could not have been lost on her. Sarah Orne Jewett's "The White Heron," the story of the influence of a noble pine tree and a rare and beautiful bird upon a child's spirit, was a favorite of Mrs. Freeman's. Indeed, both she and Miss Jewett go beyond Hawthorne—to whom both admitted a debt—in that their trees, birds, and animals are not only symbols or projections of character but also objects which interact with human personalities and are formative of character.

American literature abounds in examples of such relationships: Poe and his raven; the crew of the *Pequod* and the White Whale;

the boy, the bear, and the dog in Faulkner's famous story; the rancher and the black panther in Walter Van Tilburg Clark's *The Track of the Cat*; the woman and the flowers in Steinbeck's "Chrysanthemums"; and Santiago and the giant fish in Hemingway's *The Old Man and the Sea*. These and other stories do more than utilize fauna and flora as symbols. They use, rather, the life that surrounds man to illuminate the life of his spirit. They present this environmental life as steps and guideposts in man's voyage of self-discovery. Above all, they show how man's relationship with other living things constitutes a discipline in the personality's struggle for integration. All these uses of the world that surrounds us—not just the organic world but all of nature—were first pointed out in America by Emerson in 1836 in his essay on *Nature*. To him nature was not only a symbol of spirit, a language whereby the soul converses with itself, but a discipline of "the understanding in intellectual truths" and of the reason (intuition) in moral truths. American literature had no more skillful nor convincing exponent of these principles, still a force in our culture, than Mary Wilkins Freeman.

III *Intercontinental Tournament*

In 1907 the New York *Herald* conceived a circulation-building stunt without parallel in literary history—an Anglo-American novel-writing competition in which Mrs. Freeman would represent the United States and Max Pemberton would represent England. Not only was this to be a contest between nations but a duel between two schools of fiction as well. Mrs. Freeman was to write a "realistic tale of New England," *The Shoulders of Atlas*, which would be pitted against Pemberton's "swashbuckling romance of Old England." Installments of each were to be printed weekly in the *Herald* Sunday edition. The readers were invited to vote each week on their preference, using ballots printed in the newspaper. The winner in a final cumulative count would receive $5,000. In the full-page announcement of the contest in the magazine section of the *Herald*, an illustration depicted Mrs. Freeman mounted on a prancing white American Pegasus facing John Bull astride a black charger. As it turned out, to write her book, which would number about a hundred thousand words, Mrs. Freeman had only two months. She was doubtless spurred into this grueling assignment by the need of money to build a

$20,000 house that she and her husband were planning. The prize, which she easily won, plus serial and book rights netted her exactly this sum. The novel was the most profitable of her literary ventures.

An undisputed financial success, by any standards, *The Shoulders of Atlas*, despite the pressure under which it was written and the ballyhoo accompanying its publication, possessed more literary merit than any novel that she wrote after her marriage. Its tone is genuinely realistic, if one overlooks the final chapter with its multiple weddings. The plot, though bordering on melodrama, is believable. Foster's accusation that it hinges too much on a "hocus-pocus of concealed and altered wills and melodramatic poisoning"[2] is not tenable. The suspicion that a schoolteacher of doubtful moral character who has died of heart failure was actually murdered by poisoning exists only in the minds of the pettier and more neurotic townspeople, where such suspicions are always spawned. Neither the police nor the responsible citizens believe it. As for the wills, in fact only one is concealed and it has not been altered. It has no legal validity since it has not been signed, and it was superseded by another completely legal one.

The only conflict arising from the existence of the two wills is in the mind of the heroine, Sylvia Whitman. Though she has inherited a house and some property perfectly legally from a distant cousin, her discovery of the older unsigned will works upon her New England conscience until she is convinced that she is holding what rightly belongs to the young and pretty relative mentioned in the will, Rose Fletcher, now residing with her in the inherited house. Far from being a gimmick on the part of the author, the earlier will is a stimulus that prods Sylvia's conscience into more violent activity. Long before she discovered it, she had been uneasy about the inheritance. Lacking the will, she would have found other grounds for self-accusation.

Sylvia Whitman, indeed, is one of Mrs. Freeman's New England women of indomitable volition and hypersensitive conscience. Eager to accept the legacy, which lifts her and her husband out of a lifetime of oppressive poverty, she is quick to find reasons to make herself miserable in spite of (in fact, because of) her good luck. For months, her own will is in mortal battle with her conscience. The deadlock is broken when, in accord with Puritan tradition, she makes public confession at Rose's wedding. Though informed by a lawyer present that she holds the property legally, she persists in her self-flagellation: "I was just as guilty, for I had the knowledge of sin in my heart and I held it there. I was just as guilty" (292). To this daughter of the Puritans the knowledge of sin was sweeter than that of innocence.

More than any of Mrs. Freeman's other novels *The Shoulders of Atlas* dwells upon the psychic abnormalities latent in the New England village. Sylvia's morbidly sensitive conscience is, of course, nothing new. But her attachment to Rose, though she herself regards it as maternal, is unmistakably homosexual. She is physically attracted to the girl, to the pinkness and softness of her flesh; insists on undressing her at bed-time, though Rose is a grown woman; restrains herself only with great exertion from embraces far from maternal; and fights her marriage with hysterical ferocity. The desire to keep the girl is as strong as the desire to keep the money, which she erroneously thinks belongs to the girl. Miss Eliza Farrell, the schoolteacher supposedly poisoned by her landlady, is even more obviously homosexual. Not a "Miss" at all, she has been married but was deserted by her husband shortly after the wedding. Now aging, she desperately tries to retain her beauty with cosmetics. Though she seems anxious to attract men, she excites their repulsion rather than admiration: "She loved women better than a woman usually does, and women could not abide her" (78).

In East Westland, the village in which *The Shoulders of Atlas* is laid, neurosis of sexual origin is endemic. Hysteria is as rife as in seventeenth-century Salem, where sexual jealousies and frustrations—at least according to Mrs. Freeman's *Giles Corey*—vied with religious fear and bigotry in producing abnormal behavior. In East Westland, the death of the disturbing Rose Farrell under slightly suspicious circumstances catches the imagination of the oversexed Lucy Ayres. She attempts to feed poison candy to Eliza Fletcher, who is her rival for the affections of the young principal of the local high school. In a novel written after 1920 Lucy would have been depicted as a nymphomaniac, which she latently was. But her position in a respectable family in a strait-laced New England town completely frustrates her supercharged libido and forces her into pathological conduct. Her presence in the town was as provocative to the men as Rose Farrell's homosexuality was upsetting to the women. Though Lucy's efforts at poisoning are pitifully ineffective, Eliza's lover —the high-school principal—and other males close to her succumb to irrational fear and take irrational action in their efforts to protect her.

The causation that Mrs. Freeman ascribes to the hysteria of Lucy and to some extent to the abnormality of Miss Farrell is essentially deterministic—a point of view that was becoming increasingly noticeable in her books after 1900. The thesis of *The Shoulders of Atlas* is that every human being groans under some almost unbearable burden that Atlas himself could support only with the greatest difficulty. Some of these burdens, like Sylvia's sense of guilt, the sufferer may have a fair chance of removing, or at least lightening, by his own efforts. But others, like Miss Farrell's and Lucy Ayer's sexual compulsions are beyond the individual's control. Either one learns to bear them or succumbs, as did Lucy, who becomes temporarily insane. Such a burden, as Lucy's mother says, "may bend innocence into guilt and modesty into shamelessness, but there is no more reason for condemnation than in a case of typhoid fever" (178).

But sex is not the sole deterministic force in the destinies of the villagers of East Westland. As always, Mrs. Freeman is alive to the miseries of the poor, whether unable to work or chained to a life-devouring factory treadmill. The elderly Henry Whitman, an operative in shoe mills since boyhood, is physically and psychologically unable to enjoy the leisure afforded him by his wife's inheritance of six hundred dollars a year. Whereas her enjoyment of this princely income is spoiled by a Puritan conscience, his is rendered impossible by the habit of work. Against Sylvia's wishes, he surreptitiously takes back his job. Intelligent enough to be bitter about what economic exploitation has done to him, he cannot force himself out of the old pattern of bondage. Henry is one of a lengthy roster of characters in Mrs. Freeman's books who have been defeated by the social system and who suffer the acute agony of realizing how cruelly their days have been wasted and yet know there is nothing they can do to alter matters. Members of this dismal kinship are found in *Jerome*, in *The Portion of Labor*, and in *By the Light of the Soul.*

V *A Cooperative Novel*

What with the Anglo-American contest and the experiment with melodrama, this was a time of literary showmanship for Mrs. Freeman. Equally bizarre was her part in a stunt dreamed up by *Harper's Magazine* in what one critic termed "pure vaudeville." The two stars in the act were Howells and Henry James; the supporting talent included, among others, Elizabeth Stuart Phelps, Alice Brown, Henry Van Dyke, and Mary Wilkins Freeman. The show was entitled *The Whole Family*, a cooperative novel, appearing as a serial in *Harper's* and later in book form. The completed novel consists of twelve chapters, each by a different author; and each presents in the first person various members, and a friend, of an upstate New York family. Howells presents the father; Henry James, a married son. Mary Wilkins Freeman was assigned the role of a foolishly romantic maiden aunt who vies with her niece for the affections of a man young enough to be her child. A sampling of the chapters reveals an amazing uniformity of style and a consistent, though not very lofty, level of literary skill. James's chapter carries the stamp of the famous later manner but the others blend together uncannily. Mrs. Freeman's depiction of spinsterish vanity and folly is neither superior nor inferior to the other chapters.

CHAPTER *10*

The End of a Career; Reputation

THE FICTION discussed in the previous chapter represents Mrs. Freeman's rather desperate efforts to find fresh subjects and genres. Along with this experimentation, she kept up a constant output of stories and novels of a more conventional or commonplace sort. In these works the decline in quality that marked her Jersey years is painfully apparent. Her transplantation from Randolph, still a country village, to suburban Metuchen put her at a disadvantage. Her best writing had always been about rural life and people; in her new environment, she was without the material she could handle most effectively.

I The Debtor

The two longest novels of this period, *The Debtor* (1905) and *By the Light of the Soul* (1906), have their settings wholly or in part in a New York suburb like Metuchen. Both were published by Harper and Brothers, first in serialized form and later as books, and thus presumably met the literary standards of this highly respected publisher. Yet *The Debtor*, laid entirely in Jersey, is essentially a silly story. Some of the intentional humor, to be sure, comes off reasonably well. One can smile at the wiles of the four-flusher Carroll, not an uncommon suburban type, as he dupes the tradespeople of Banbridge. These townsfolk are, of course, the "natives," the residents from long before the commuters moved in; and, as such, Mrs. Freeman, the specialist in village character, makes them come to life. Most likable is Anderson, a lawyer turned grocer, a bachelor approaching middle age, who marries Carroll's daughter Charlotte. Charlotte herself, however, is enough to spoil a whole book. A simpering nincompoop, she is the product of a degree of sentimentality that Mrs.

Freeman had hitherto not displayed. More realistically conceived is Carroll's hatred for the business rival who has ruined him—a hatred so consuming that it becomes directed against himself and, in accord with the Freudian theory of suicide, almost leads him to take his own life. But an occasional psychological insight and several amusing and lifelike characters are not enough to salvage over five hundred pages of fiction blemished by pervasive mawkishness and a preposterous plot. By any standards, *The Debtor* is a failure. By the standards of Mrs. Freeman's best fiction, it is an abysmal failure.

II By the Light of the Soul

More can be said for *By the Light of the Soul*, an undertaking of some two hundred thousand words. The title indicates the novel's theme—the Emersonian notion that the soul in itself is a source of insight adequate to guide us through the moral labyrinths of life. Friends of Mrs. Freeman considered the book to be a spiritual autobiography. The heroine, Maria Edgham, in her childhood is a replica of the child Mary Wilkins—a pretty, bright, somewhat spoiled, intensely sensitive girl. The religious growth of Maria, who was born into a New Jersey commuting family but was of New England stock on her mother's side, suggests her creator's tendency to combine a fairly orthodox Calvinism with a rather amorphous but apparently satisfying mysticism.

Learning as a young girl of her father's mortal illness, Maria mildly rebels against the God who serves so treacherously those who have kept their covenant with Him. Without ceasing to attend church, she retains certain reservations concerning the God of her fathers. As life closes in on her, she experiences, first, feelings of her utter insignificance in the vast natural scheme of things as revealed on starry winter nights and, later, in times of real crisis, a conviction that she is as necessary to God as He is to her in a universe of which the foundation is love. Impelled by this belief, she achieves prodigious feats of selflessness in bringing happiness to her sister Evelyn.

Some readers have termed Maria Edgham a bore. Truly her dreary, unwavering seriousness, her will that can ruthlessly smother her most turbulent emotions, if these in any way threaten to lead her from the straitest path of duty, her morbidly acute conscience, her fiercely determined charitableness towards the poor, and above all her readiness to condemn all others who fall short of her own superhuman standards—all these traits are tiresome. As Mrs. Freeman frequently states, Maria comes from a long line of females of indomitable will. In her assurance of the rightness of her own views and acts Maria doubtlessly resembles an old-time Puritan convinced of membership in the community of saints. Yet in her moments of mystical transport as well as in her loyalty to her family, Maria is not totally obnoxious. Certainly Mrs. Freeman did not mean her to be.

One reason Maria becomes a bit ludicrous to the reader is that the plot of the novel provides only the feeblest motivation for her powers of will and endurance. The central device is a marriage, never consummated, that a dull-witted parson forced on her and a high-school classmate while the two were wandering in New York City in search of Maria's little sister who had run away from home. Such a marriage, even if legal to begin with—which is doubtful, since no license had been secured—could have been annulled without the slightest difficulty and with dishonor to no one. Yet the couple, who understandably hate each other and seldom thereafter even nod to each other in the street, carry their secret with them far into adulthood, abandoning any thought of real marriage with other partners. Inevitably, of course, Maria's younger sister Evelyn falls in love with Maria's "husband"; and equally inevitably this occurs at the moment, deferred for fifteen years, when Maria and her spouse are beginning to be attracted to each other and are on the verge of entering into actual union. Maria's will power and sense of duty surge. She flees, changes her name, gets a report printed that she is dead. The sister is free to marry her "brother-in-law," and she does so. In the context of such tomfoolery, Maria's otherwise impressive and valid, if repelling, strength of character becomes unconvincing and irrelevant.

Yet even this novel is not totally without strength. It catches the atmosphere of the New Jersey commuting town in which the first half is laid. Shifting to a Massachusetts mill city, as if Mrs. Freeman were seeking more familiar ground, the action becomes more credible; and the setting continues to be interesting, especially the glimpses of the decay and demoralization in which people on the undesirable side of the river live. Prostitution, drunkenness, and criminal neglect of children are presented with a "naturalism" that either Crane or Dreiser would find to his taste.

In *By the Light of the Soul*, Mrs. Freeman voices more outspokenly then ever before her awareness of the folly of mankind. As in many of her works, there is a character who takes petty reprisals against destiny for assigning him to a distasteful life, in this case life in a run-down industrial town: "He, Henry Stillman, actually had a conviction that he was showing recrimination and wounding fate, which had so injured him, if only with a pinprick, by staying away from church" (235). In earlier stories, characters who rebel against fate—the woman in "A Tardy Thanksgiving"—retain some dignity; but Henry, as he thumbs his nose at God by reading scandal sheets during church hours, merely makes himself ridiculous.

Despite his folly, Henry through the years has acquired a bitter realization of the weakness of humanity. Was Mrs. Freeman's marriage with an alcoholic bringing her to a similarly grim knowledge? Was she perhaps regretting her plunge into matrimony in her late middle age? At any rate she mercilessly lampoons the elderly spinster, Maria Stillman, otherwise a sensible woman, for her clumsy machinations to ensnare the husband of her dead sister. Likewise, the widower shows himself equally foolish in succumbing at length to a beautiful but passionless schoolteacher who is incapable of loving even her own daughter. In this woman, indeed, there is an exhibit of will-less amorality as inevitable as any act of nature; for she "was, after all, as she was made, a being on a very simple and primitive plan, with an acute perception of her own welfare and . . . as innocently self-seeking as a butterfly or a honeybee. She had never seen anybody in the world except herself. She had been born humanity blind, and it was possibly no more her fault than if she had been born with a hump" (374).

In allowing themselves to be victimized by such predators men are, of course, weak; but in Mrs. Freeman's own childhood home, as well as in most of her books, merciless female domination of spineless males was the rule. Yet in this novel the married men seem more discontented, more disillusioned than ever before. One scorns them rather than sympathizes with them—which was becoming more and more Mrs. Freeman's feeling about her fellow mortals. She was approaching Mark Twain's indignation against "the damned human race." In addition to folly, she reveals in *By the Light of the Soul* behavior describable only as gratuitous malice. When a girl runs away, the neighbors secretly gloat while they pretend to comfort the mother; and when a school-girl is jilted by her lover, her classmates covertly exult.

III *Afterglow*

Mrs. Freeman had always done her best writing in short fiction. During the New Jersey years she continued to pound through her typewriter a steady flow of stories. Of these an occasional one ranked with the best she had written, but the days of whole volumes of distinguished tales were past. Only a brief glance at these later collections is worthwhile.

The Givers (1904) is composed largely of Christmas stories, competent in their evocation of New England settings, especially of the blizzards and gales of December, and in their characterization. But they are sentimental in plot, as is not unusual for their genre. Yet few even of these are downright mawkish. The male and female solitaries who people them do, of course, have joy brought into their dreary existences in accord with the season—but the joy is always a lasting one, involving basic transformations of their lives. For example, two feuding spinster sisters get together after years of estrangement; a lonely hill farmer finally marries the girl who had jilted him decades before; and, like true New Englanders, these people take their good fortune without undue display of emotion. Studies in generosity, the stories are at worst harmless and, at best, heartwarming. As its title indicates, the volume, including the stories not on the Christmas theme, celebrates the human race as givers —of material goods, of affection, and even of reputation, as in "The Last Gift," which tells how an impoverished minister steals to give to the poor. To brand such stories as being untrue to life, in their spirit at least, would be misanthropy in the extreme. Mrs. Freeman has elsewhere exposed human meanness frequently enough to exonerate her from the accusation of being a pollyanna.

In 1907 appeared *The Fair Lavinia and Others*, a volume of tales with titles like "Amarina's Roses," "Eglantina," and "The Willow-Ware," and dealing for the most part with small-town gentlefolk. Though originally printed in *Harper's New Monthly*, these tales are pretty much without substance. The only exception is "The Gold," laid in Revolutionary days, and telling the story of a farmer who has a goldsmith convert his inherited precious metal into andirons, doorknobs, drawer handles, and the like, which he puts to their normal use about his house just as if they were made of brass. Having murdered the goldsmith, who alone knows what has been done with the gold, the farmer goes off to the army, refusing to tell his wife where the treasure is hidden. The wife ransacks the house and digs up every square foot of the farm. Eventually, she is murdered by marauders seeking the supposed hoard. The farmer at last returns and lives out his days in poverty surrounded by wealth he dare not, and will not, use. As a tale of greed that destroys a human soul, this story is powerful. The final scene, when neighbors break into the farmhouse one icy winter day and find the old miser dead before his fireplace hearth with the andirons and doorknobs glittering in the cold sunlight, is comparable to the scene of Judge Pyncheon's death in *The House of the Seven Gables.*

The next collection, *The Winning Lady and Others* (1909), was considered by some to be the best that Mrs. Freeman had published—an estimate that is unfounded. First, in all her later stories and novels, Mrs. Freeman's style was gaining fluency and complexity at the expense of the unadorned simplicity and directness that had contributed so much to the effectiveness of her earlier work. Glibness was supplanting feeling and was hanging like a veil between the author and her material. Second, in these Jersey years Mrs. Freeman's separation from rural New England, the source of all that is worthwhile in her work, was making itself felt more and more. In these later volumes, a return to her old subject matter, in spirit if not in body, usually meant a renewal of her writing strength.

Thus in *The Winning Lady*, the title piece with its bridge-playing suburban "ladies," is extremely feeble. The next two stories, "Little-Girl-Afraid-of-a-Dog" and "The Joy of Youth," with village settings, recount poignantly lifelike episodes in a country girl's growing up. Most impressive of all in the collection is "Old Woman Magoun," which tells how a proud old country-woman lets her dead daughter's illegitimate child eat the berries of deadly nightshade and die rather than permit her to be taken by her father, the degenerate son of a once respectable family. As a study in rural degeneracy, the story is unsurpassed in Mrs. Freeman's writing. Finally, a piece with a small town, rather than a village or rural setting, deserves attention. "The Selfishness of Amelia Lamkin" focuses upon a New England conscience that literally kills its possessor. Amelia has been so bent on self-sacrifice in doing her duty that she has refused help offered by others of her numerous family. In her search for duties to fulfill, she has mortally exhausted herself; and, ironically, she has converted selflessness into selfishness. Her daughter's launching into a similar course of solipsism points to the cultural-hereditary nature of the syndrome.

In 1912 Harper published Mrs. Freeman's *The Yates Pride*, a tiny volume, exhibiting the haughtiness of a well-born maiden who is forced to take in laundry but delivers it in a baby carriage so that "folks" will not know what she is doing. The neighbors think she has adopted a baby, but so formidable is Miss Eudora Yates that they don't ask her. Eudora's lover returns after an absence of many years, and he also assumes that she has adopted a child. He asks her to marry him, forgetting the arrogant rebuff he had taken from her years ago. She then scurries around to find a baby she can really adopt, and finally accepts her lover's offer. The story is effectively told from the point of view of gossips—at least at the beginning—gathered in a house across the street from Miss Yates's, on whom they spy by peeking from behind the curtains.

Also in 1912 appeared *The Butterfly House*, an attempt to satirize the pettinesses of life in a New Jersey suburb. Understandably, the reviewers found the novel to be evidence of a serious decline in its author's powers. The satire, which centers upon the doings of clubwomen, is dull; and the plot, which hinges upon one woman's posing as the author of another woman's anonymously published best-selling novel, is preposterous without being humorous. But the depiction of the utter selfishness of the impostor, who psychologically is "obliged to commit an ignoble deed in order to render her soul capable of tasting to the full . . ." (221), is effective. Her later remorse and her desire for confession, which she lacks the strength to go through with, suggest rather poignantly the tortured consciences that Mrs. Freeman so successfully dissected in her former work. But these glimmerings are in no way sufficient to redeem an almost total failure.

The Copy-Cat and Other Stories (1914) contains the last stories of merit that Mrs. Freeman wrote. The first six are about children in an unnamed village, apparently suburban but with many rural characteristics. The children are real, "as chokeful of mischief as a pod of peas" (64). Several of them appear in more than one story, as do some of the adults. The series provides a view of village life as lived by youngsters, and this life, as Mrs. Freeman depicts it, is much less fraught with the clash of wills and eruption of passions than that of the adult villagers in her usual story. Avoiding sentimentality, these tales underscore the wholesomeness of small-town childhood, but the children are for the most part of prosperous families in a prosperous community that sends its progeny to a private school. In earlier collections or novels, for example *Jerome*, Mrs. Freeman presented the spectacle of childhood blighted by extreme poverty, both of spirit and of things.

In addition to truly delightful stories of childhood, *The Copy-Cat* contains several other pieces of a quality that marks a real, if brief, resurgence of Mrs. Freeman's talents. Among these are two stories of revolt. "Dear Annie" tells of a young woman's rebellion against exploitation by her sister and by her weak-willed father, the village minister. Mild-natured Annie finally walks out of the family circle and lives alone across the street in a dwelling she has inherited from her grandmother. For a year, strengthened in her purpose by her sister's attempts to turn her lover against her, she withstands the whimpering importunities of her family. Less sensational than "The Revolt of Mother," the story is more effective because it records a plausible spiritual growth, over an extended period, both in Annie and in her relatives.

The other story of revolt, "The Balking of Christopher," is one of the loveliest things Mrs. Freeman ever wrote. In it the revolt is not against another person or a family but against God and the duty orthodox religion enjoins. All his life Christopher had attempted to do his duty, and Providence had always thrown obstacles in his way—fire, drought, flood, sickness, death. One spring morning Christopher decides he will not do his duty, which that day is to plough the South Field. Instead he goes to the minister to ask a question: "Why did I come into the world without any choice?" (275). This is an age-old question and a justifiable one, especially among Puritans with their legalistic concept of reciprocal obligations between God and man. Man does his part; why does not God do His? God brings man into the world, bids him to obey the law, and then hinders him in every way from achieving obedience. In many instances Mrs. Freeman had questioned the wisdom of devoting a life solely to duty, and she does so again in this story.

When Christopher announces his future course, the minister listens sympathetically. His plan is to leave the farm for a time to live in solitude in a sugaring shack far up on a mountainside and to enjoy the changing seasons as his farming duties have never permitted him to do. Nothing will swerve this unlettered Thoreau from his purpose. Leaving his house and wife, he resides on the mountain. The minister, fascinated by the venture, periodically visits him, bringing supplies of food. But after a few months Christopher comes down from the mountain, saying, "I've got rested from my whole life" (290). He is settled in his mind now, he tells the minister. He will never complain again, no matter what happens. He has found "that all the good things and all the bad things that come to a man who tries to do right are just to prove to him that he is on the right path . . . [and] I have found out the answer to my 'Why?' . . . I have found out that the only way to heaven for the children of men is through the earth" (290). Christopher's revolt has turned into acquiescence, which Mrs. Freeman elsewhere has hinted at as the most perfect form of freedom (in "Silence," for example). But such acceptance must not be supine; it is won through a grappling with problems—not in blindly, doggedly forcing oneself into duty simply because it is the will of God.

An Alabaster Box, the final novel to bear Mrs. Freeman's name on its title page, was written in collaboration with Florence Morse Kingsley. It elicited from one reviewer the remark that Mrs. Freeman stood in need of re-establishing her reputation and from another the comment that she would do better to avoid collaboration in the future. While a sorry excuse indeed for a novel, *An Alabaster Box* is interesting as a final statement of some of Mrs. Freeman's attitudes. The plot, though improbable, is simple: Mr. Andrew Bolton, a banker in the village of Brookville, embezzles money entrusted to him, goes to jail for his crime, but does not make good the grievous losses suffered by the townspeople. His little daughter is left in the care of an uncle, who later dies and leaves her a considerable fortune. True to her Puritan heritage, the daughter takes upon herself some of her father's guilt; she returns, as a young woman, to Brookville to live incognito in her father's old house and to lavish benefits upon the villagers in restitution for the wrong her father did them. Her father, broken in mind and body after eighteen years in prison, comes home to live with her immediately after his release. But Brookville has become as sick as the man who wronged it—not, as the minister explains, "because of Andrew Bolton's crime [,] but because Brookville had never forgiven Andrew Bolton. Hate is the one destructive element in the universe. . . . It is impossible for a man or woman who hates another to prosper. . . . God is love—the opposite of hate. Hence all Power is enlisted on the side of *love* . . ." (298-99). About the hatred of the villagers there can be no doubt: they descend upon the Bolton house and stone it, driving the old man into the woods, where he dies of starvation and exposure. As an indictment of the corporate meanness of a small town, *An Alabaster Box* is as bitter as Mark Twain's *The Man That Corrupted Hadleyburg* though decidedly weaker in ironic effect, characterization, and style.

Mrs. Freeman's last collection of short fiction, *Edgewater People* (1918), is also her poorest. Purporting to be a study of the process of growth of four villages that are the offshoot of one ancient settlement, the book is actually a loosely connected series of stories that happen to have their setting in the same area. Certain characters reappear several times, but their presence in no way demonstrates Mrs. Freeman's contention that communities, like individuals, inherit identical qualities from a common forebear. "I may have succeeded in making this evident in this volume," she writes in the Preface. "I may have failed" (2). Unfortunately, she failed. One need not even name the five communities—the parent one and the four offspring—about which she writes, for they are all without any interesting characteristics, individually or together. The most notable character in the volume, Sarah Edgewater, is a mere distorted echo of the strong-willed New England women who had populated Mrs. Freeman's earlier work. The subject of one of the stories,

Sarah's conquering a pathological fear of loneliness by transforming her hate and resentment towards her sister into love, is psychologically convincing as an idea but not as it is developed in this instance. The idea was infinitely better handled in *Pembroke.* Equally pathetic as an echo is "Value Received," based on the theme that one who gives has a sacred duty to receive from the giver in turn. As presented in "Old Lady Pingree" in *A Humble Romance* the theme had cogency, as it also did in "The Selfishness of Amelia Lamkin." As developed in "Value Received," by methods not worth mentioning, it is ludicrous. But most distressing of all in the volume is the blind chauvinism evident in several of the stories, notably "Both Cheeks," in which the conversion of a pacifist into a blood-thirsty militarist is presented as the ultimate in spiritual growth.

As with many a person of less than first-rate intellect, World War I brought out all the second-rate in Mrs. Freeman. The first line of a poem she contributed to a volume called *America in the War* (1918), edited by Louis Raemakers, is sufficient evidence: "America wakes! The White Christ has called her. . . ." The war was, of course, only a secondary influence in Mrs. Freeman's artistic collapse. Her age (almost seventy), the exhausting drainage of her energies during forty years of fantastically prolix writing, and her husband's alcoholism merging into psychosis—these are reasons enough for artistic bankruptcy. No more volumes and only a handful of fugitive pieces appeared during the last twelve years of her life.

But the 1920's held several honors for her. On April 23, 1926, the American Academy of Letters awarded her the Howells Medal for distinction in fiction. The presentation was made by Hamlin Garland, an old acquaintance of hers, who characterized her work as "an unparalleled record of New England life."[1] On November 10 of the same year she was among the first four women ever to be elected to the National Institute of Arts and Letters. The other three were Agnes Repplier, Margaret Deland, and Edith Wharton. For the next four years she suffered from deteriorating health, and on March 15, 1930, she died at the age of seventy-seven.

IV *Reputation*

With *A Humble Romance* and *A New England Nun* Mrs. Freeman established a reputation that endured throughout her life and only in the past decades has shown signs of serious decline. Reviews of her work over a period of forty years were overwhelmingly favorable. Prototypal of her press notices is that in the London *Spectator* on *A New England Nun*: "The stories are among the most remarkable feats of what we may call literary impressionism in our language, so powerfully do they stamp on the reader's mind the image of the classes of individuals they portray without spending on the picture a single redundant word, a single superfluous word."[2] Holmes and Lowell and, as we have seen, Howells and James were admirers of the vividness and power of her stories in the 1890's. Enhancing her transatlantic reputation was an article entiled "Un Romancier de la Nouvelle-Angleterre," by the French author Madame Thérèse Blanc-Bentzon, in the *Revue des Deux Mondes* (August, 1896).

Writing over the signature Th. Bentzon, the Frenchwoman, who was a personal friend of Sarah Orne Jewett and who later wrote several books on America, found in Miss Wilkins *une âme* as strange as that of a Russian or a Scandinavian. No Frenchman could ever fully comprehend *Pembroke*, for example, with its presumption of the continuing "reign" of the Bible. In Miss Wilkins, in fact, she finds lingering the spirit of seventeenth-century England—its consciousness of sin and its reference of all activities to a "spiritual end." She thinks that Miss Wilkins lacks the artistic delicacy of Mrs. Stowe and the imagination of Miss Jewett, but that she enjoys a spontaneity of expression, a strong sense of realism, a poetic talent (Mme. Blanc-Bentzon cites "A Far-Away Melody"), and a painter's skill that enables her to sketch a landscape in one or two strokes.

For years, of course, Miss Wilkins had basked in the recognition accorded her by the Harper periodicals. Not only did Harper's publish most of what she wrote, but the company also promoted her reputation with highly favorable editorial comments on her work. Less biased, perhaps, was the recognition conferred on her by the *Atlantic Monthly*, which in May, 1899, printed one of the most comprehensive and profound analyses of her fiction ever to appear. The title of the article was "Miss Wilkins: an Idealist in Masquerade." The author, Charles Miner Thompson, traces in some detail the influence of Miss Wilkins' Puritan background on her fiction with its preoccupation with abnormal volition. He draws the inevitable analogy with Hawthorne, and he correctly designates her as a pathologist of diseases of the will. In her style he sees a marked improvement between her early simplicity and the fluency beginning with *Silence*—a conclusion that few would share in. Finally, he shrewdly detects beneath her "realism" the Emersonian idealist who has had a vision of the mystical beneath the drab exteriors of her villagers and farmfolk.

In the same year, 1899, the *Atlantic* carried Rollin Lynde Hartt's article, "A New England Hill Town," in which Miss Wilkins was cited for the accuracy of her observations of society and individuals in the back country. Her reputation as a writer, a psychologist, and a social historian was firmly established. It is not surprising, then, to find Paul Elmer More seriously comparing her with Hawthorne in an essay written for *Independent* (July, 1904) and later included in *Shelburne Essays*, Second Series. The essay, "Hawthorne: Looking Before and After," places Mrs. Freeman chronologically last in a line of Puritan writers beginning with Cotton Mather and including Hawthorne as its greatest figure. Mrs. Freeman, he maintains, presented the final stage of the isolating and dehumanizing tendencies in the Calvinist culture of New England—a stage of spiritual impotence and despair but one that was ripe for an eruption back into some sort of humanism. The first sign of this reorientation to humanity he saw in *Jerome*, a novel which he considered her best long work. The nadir of impotency he thought was recorded in "Two Old Lovers," which he analyzed at length.

Among academic literati Fred Lewis Pattee gave Mrs. Freeman the first and most extended serious attention in *A History of American Literature Since 1870* (1915) and in "On the Terminal Moraine of New England Puritanism" in *Side-Lights on American Literature* (1922). Though he views Mrs. Freeman as a realist of the Hardy, Flaubert, and Howells variety (the juxtapositions are the critic's), Pattee otherwise sees pretty much eye to eye with Charles Miner Thompson, from whom he may have derived most of his ideas. Mrs. Freeman is the anatomist of the Puritan will, the recorder of the last gasp of the old theocracy, the laureate of New England's decline.

For the next fifteen years Mrs. Freeman's literary stock remained firm. In 1915 Howells used her work as a touchstone by which to assess Frost's *A Boy's Will* and *North of Boston.* Blanche Colton Williams in *Our Short Story Writers* (1926) devoted over twenty pages to her life, art, and methods of work; and she concluded that her best stories will endure as evocations of a place and an era. John Macy in "The Passing of the Yankee," published in *The Bookman* (August 1931) shortly after Mrs. Freeman's death and on the three hundredth anniversary of the founding of Boston, considered Mrs. Freeman's work before 1900 among the outstanding memorials to a vanishing way of life. Less general were F. O. Matthiessen's comments in the same year in an article titled "New England Stories." Among American writers, Matthiessen found Mrs. Freeman "unsurpassed . . . in her ability to give the breathless intensity of a moment" (406); and he caught in her work a deep sense of the tragic dimension of life—a Melvillean awareness of the darker side of human nature. "The struggle of the heart to live by its own strength alone is her constant theme, and the sudden revolt of a spirit that will endure no more from circumstance provides her most stirring dramas" (408). He pointed out parallels between Mrs. Freeman's life and works and those of Emily Brontë, on whom, indeed, Mrs. Freeman had written a perceptive essay.

Matthiessen's remarks echo—very likely unknowingly—ideas expressed a generation earlier by the British critic Arthur Machen in a volume called *Hieroglyphics: a Note upon Ecstasy in Literature.* Machen's thesis is that fine literature concerns itself solely with the expression of ecstasy; all else is merely reading matter, though, to Machen, this inferior category includes the works of such luminaries as Jane Austen, George Eliot, and Thackeray. Ecstasy Machen defines as the expression of, or contact with, the *other self* (which is usually unconscious) —that is, with the spiritual, eternal, supernatural side of man. "There is a world elsewhere; its speech is called poetry" (viii), poetry not necessarily being metrical language. Machen classifies much of Mrs. Freeman's work prior to 1900 as literature of ecstasy, mainly because of the impression of remoteness and loneliness that pervades her pages. Loneliness "is merely another synonym for that property [ecstasy] which makes the difference between real literature and reading-matter. . . . So this is my plea for Miss Wilkins. I think that she has indicated the condition of 'ecstasis'; she has painted a society, indeed, but a society in which each man stands apart, responsible only for himself and to himself, conscious only of himself and his God. . . . This doctrine of awful, individual loneliness prevails so far that it is carried into the necessary and ordinary transactions of social life, often with results that are very absurd" (173-75). But to Machen the presence of absurdity in no way invalidates Mrs. Freeman's work, any more than it would to an existentialist. The exercise of the individual's will, in solitude, choosing its own direction and creating its possessor's very being, is the important thing—not whether the resultant action is prudent or absurd. Thus Machen insists that even Marcus Woodman's farcical sit-in on the church steps for ten years ("A Conflict Ended") serves as "a witness to the everlasting truth that, at last, each man must stand or fall alone, and that if he would stand he must, to a certain extent, live alone with his own soul" (176).

Most anthologies of American literature, especially those of the short story, contain at least one selection from Mrs. Freeman's pen. Usually her contribution stands side by side with one from Sarah Orne Jewett. In general the accompanying commentaries, when they engage in criticism at all, concur with the verdict given by Carlos Baker in *The Literary History of the United States.* Carlos Baker considers Miss Jewett and Mrs. Freeman the best artists among the delineators of New England life and character. Miss Jewett was able to sustain her art at a higher level, he thinks, but Mrs. Freeman at her best was her equal. Moreover, in the first two collections of Mrs. Freeman's stories he discovers "a sharpness of line and directness of purpose . . . which even Miss Jewett could not match" (847). In certain of her stories he believes "there is a suggestion of hidden sublimations of which a Freudian might have made much" (848).

Excepting Edward Foster's biography *Mary E. Wilkins Freeman* (1956) the most recent extensive treatment of Mrs. Freeman is that of Van Wyck Brooks in *New England: Indian Summer.* Only the early part of her career lies within the scope of the book, but Brooks, in the ten or eleven pages he devotes to her, presents her as one of the major exhibits of the culture he is attempting to depict. To him, Miss Wilkins' tales are "plain, stark, factual" transcriptions of the realities of a region's decadence, worthy of comparison with O'Neill's *Mourning Becomes Electra*—and, perhaps, *Desire Under the Elms*. "There was something fierce and primitive in her view of life, and the Furies existed for her . . ." (464). He, too, attributes to her a tragic vision, a profundity growing from "the grand inheritance of the Puritan faith" (464). Like most later critics, Van Wyck Brooks, gives only brief mention to her novels; but of her short fiction, he concludes that "in some of her early tales, perhaps twenty or thirty, she was an eminent artist, as eminent as Miss Jewett, and even more so, because of the depth of feeling that informed her art" (465).

It will be noted that most of the critics cited in this chapter and earlier perceive in Mrs. Freeman's best work something more than "local color." Whether the special quality is called tragic vision, profundity, or ecstasy, there has been general agreement since 1890 onward that, though she presents an ample canvas of the New England village in all its detail, she also bathes her subject in tints of universality and eternity. She has succeeded in conveying a sense of the human condition—the human condition in its New England manifestations. Writing in *The American Scene* (1907), Henry James remarks that in New England the landscape seemed to be uttering a plea: not so much, "Live upon me and thrive by me," as, "Live *with* me, somehow, and let us make out together what we may do for each other—something that is not merely estimable in more or less greasy greenbacks . . ." (20). In the writing of Mrs. Freeman the countrymen are struggling—not always unsuccessfully—to answer this plea. To repeat Sarah Orne Jewett's words, "The stories of strange lives have been whispered to the earth, their thoughts have burned themselves into the cold rocks."

A writer therefore with universal overtones but with microscopic focus upon one area of the nation, Mrs. Freeman represents regionalism at its very best. Nor is the region that engages her talents a negligible backwater in American culture. It is one that was seminal and transcontinentally influential in forming the American character and in establishing the national values. No major Northern author of the nineteenth century failed to realize this function of New England. Harriet Beecher Stowe's remarks in the preface to *Oldtown Folks* are only slightly colored by regional chauvinism: "New England has been to these United States what the Dorian hive was to Greece. It has always been a capital country to emigrate from, and North, South, East, and West have been populated largely from New England, so that the seed-bed of New England was the seed-bed of this great American Republic, and of all that is likely to come of it" (iii).

The most recent among comments on Mary Wilkins Freeman is Sylvia Townsend Warner's "Item, One Empty House" in the *New Yorker* (March 26, 1966). A mood piece—half story, half essay—it recounts the British author's experience as a house guest in Connecticut. Most of what she knows of New England is what she has read in novels and stories, especially those of Mrs. Freeman. But when she mentions Mrs. Freeman to her American literary friends, she is informed that that author is no longer held in much esteem. So she keeps her thoughts to herself, in the meanwhile indulging in reminiscences of Mrs. Freeman's work, for which she evidences a deeply sensitive and perceptive appreciation. Up before her hosts the morning after a party, she takes a walk along the snowy country roads. Her attention is attracted by an old farmhouse tall and gaunt in the whitened meadows. Approaching closer, she notices foot tracks a week or more old leading up to the door but none coming out. She had encountered a tale by Mary Wilkins—an unfinished tale.

Unlike most Americans, Sylvia Townsend Warner knows that Mrs. Freeman's New England still has its home in the American psyche. It has not yet come out—even as a corpse.

Notes and References

Chapter One

My chief sources for biographical data in this and other chapters are my own *Acres of Flint: Writers of Rural New England, 1870-1900* and Edward Foster's more detailed and comprehensive biography *Mary E. Wilkins Freeman.* For background material I have drawn not only from these sources but from a multitude of others, most notably from various works of Perry Miller and from H. F. Wilson's remarkable study, *The Hill Country of Northern New England.*

1. B. Mussey (ed.), *We Were New England* (New York, 1937), pp. 115ff.
2. Sarah Orne Jewett, *A White Heron and Other Stories* (Boston, 1892), p. 25.
3. Edward Foster, *Mary E. Wilkins Freeman* (New York, 1956), p. 14.
4. *Ibid.*, p. 9.
5. *Ibid.*, p. 30.
6. *Ibid.*, p. 51.
7. *Ibid.*, p. 53.

Chapter Two

1. Willa Cather (ed.), *The Best Short Stories of Sarah Orne Jewett* (Boston, 1925), p. xvi.
2. B. C. Williams, *Our Short Story Writers* (New York, 1926), p. 173.

Chapter Three

1. "New England in the Short Story," *Atlantic Monthly,* LXVII (June, 1891), 845-50.

Chapter Four

1. Foster, p. 31.
2. Thomas Hooker, "A True Light of Sin," in Perry Miller (ed.), *The American Puritans* (Garden City, N.Y., 1956), p. 155.
3. Urian Oakes, "The Sovereign Efficacy of Divine Providence," in *The American Puritans,* p. 206f.
4. *Ibid.*, p. 195.
5. Jonathan Edwards, *Freedom of the Will* (Andover, Mass., 1840), p. 172.

6. *Ibid.*, pp. 312-13.
7. Foster, p. 52.
8. R. W. Emerson, *The Conduct of Life* (Boston, 1904), pp. 27-28.
9. H. B. Stowe, *Poganuc People* (New York, 1878), p. 95. Much concerned with the problems of the will and predestination, Mrs. Stowe treats them at length in Chapter XXIX of *Oldtown Folks* (Boston, 1869) and in Chapter XXIII of *The Minister's Wooing* (New York, 1859). Eventually she joined the Episcopal Church, the doctrine of which on such matters seemed to her to be more rational.

Chapter Five

1. D. Sutcliffe (ed.), *Untriangulated Stars* (Cambridge, Mass., 1947), pp. 174-75.
2. Foster, pp. 134-35.

Chapter Six

1. J. G. Whittier, *Prose Works* (Boston, 1882), I, 460.
2. J. G. Whittier, *Complete Poetical Works* (Boston, 1880), p. 326.
3. T. W. Higginson, "Americanism in Literature," *Atlantic Monthly*, XXV (January, 1870), 56-63.
4. Quoted in Fred Lewis Pattee, *American Literature Since 1870* (New York, 1915), p. 229.
5. E. S. Phelps, *Chapters from a Life* (Boston, 1896), p. 263.
6. *Ibid.*, p. 264.
7. Foster, p. 89. See also Henry James's comments on Mary Wilkins Freeman in Leon Edel (ed.), *The American Essays of Henry James* (New York, 1956).

Chapter Seven

1. F. Dostoyevsky, *The Brothers Karamazov* (New York, 1950), p. 246.
2. *Ibid.*, pp. 249-50.
3. *Ibid.*, p. 256.
4. Foster, p. 154.
5. Lucy Larcom, *A New England Girlhood* (Boston, 1889), pp. 9-10.
6. Lucy Larcom, *An Idyl of Work* (Boston, 1873), p. 119.

Chapter Eight

1. Charles W. Upham, *Salem Witchcraft* (New York, 1959), II, 334.

2. *Ibid.*, II, 335-38.
3. *Ibid.*, II, 338.
4. "Giles Corey, Yeoman," *Harper's New Monthly*, LXXXVI (December, 1892), p. 38.
5. *Ibid.*, p. 38 .
6. Foster, p. 152.

Chapter Nine

1. Williams, p. 163.
2. Foster, p. 177.

Chapter Ten

1. Foster, p. 189.
2. Quoted in Fred Lewis Pattee, *Sidelights on American Literature* (New York, 1922), p. 187.

Selected Bibliography

PRIMARY SOURCES

1. *Books*

Decorative Plaques: Designs by GEORGE F. BARNES. Poems by Mary E. Wilkins. Boston: D. Lothrop and Co., [1883]. For children.

The Cow with the Golden Horns and Other Stories. Boston: D. Lothrop and Co., [1884]. For children.

The Adventures of Anne: Stories of Colonial Times. Boston: D. Lothrop and Co., [1886]. For children.

A Humble Romance and Other Stories. New York: Harper and Brothers, 1887.

A New England Nun and Other Stories. New York: Harper and Brothers, 1891.

The Pot of Gold and Other Stories. Boston: D. Lothrop and Company, [1892]. For children.

Young Lucretia and Other Stories. New York: Harper and Brothers, 1892. For children.

Jane Field. New York: Harper and Brothers, 1893. A novel.

Giles Corey, Yeoman: A Play. New York: Harper and Brothers, 1893.

Pembroke. New York: Harper and Brothers, 1894. A novel.

Comfort Pease and Her Gold Ring. New York and Chicago: Fleming H. Revell Company, 1895. For children.

Madelon. New York: Harper and Brothers, 1896. A novel.

Jerome, A Poor Man. New York: Harper and Brothers, 1897. A novel.

Once Upon a Time and Other Child-Verses. Boston: Lothrop Publishing Company, [1897].

Silence and Other Stories. New York: Harper and Brothers, 1898.

The People of Our Neighborhood. Philadelphia: Curtis Publishing Company, 1898. Stories and sketches.

The Jamesons. New York: Doubleday and McClure Company, 1899. A novel.

Evelina's Garden. New York: Harper and Brothers, 1899. (Previously printed in *Silence and Other Stories*.) A short novel.

The Heart's Highway, A Romance of Virginia. New York: Doubleday, Page and Company, 1900. A historical novel.

The Love of Parson Lord and Other Stories. New York: Harper and Brothers, 1900.

Understudies. New York: Harper and Brothers, 1901. Short stories.

The Portion of Labor. New York: Harper and Brothers, 1901. A novel.

Six Trees. New York: Harper and Brothers, 1903. Short stories.

The Wind in the Rose-Bush and Other Stories of the Supernatural. New York: Doubleday, Page and Company, 1903.
The Givers. New York: Harper and Brothers, 1904. Short stories.
The Debtor. New York: Harper and Brothers, 1905. A novel.
By the Light of the Soul. New York: Harper and Brothers, 1906. A novel.
"Doc" Gordon. New York: The Authors and Newspapers Association, 1906. A melodramatic novel.
The Fair Lavinia and Others. New York: Harper and Brothers, 1907. Short stories.
The Shoulders of Atlas. New York: Harper and Brothers, 1908. A novel.
The Whole Family, A Novel by Twelve Authors (including Mary W. Freeman, William D. Howells, Henry James, *et al.*). New York: Harper and Brothers, 1908.
The Winning Lady and Others. New York: Harper and Brothers, 1909. Short stories.
The Green Door. New York: Moffat Yard and Company, 1910. For children.
The Butterfly House. New York: Dodd, Mead and Company, 1912. A novel.
The Yates Pride: A Romance. New York: Harper and Brothers, 1912. A short novel.
The Copy-Cat and Other Stories. New York: Harper and Brothers, 1914.
An Alabaster Box (with Florence Morse Kingsley). New York: D. Appleton and Company, 1917. A novel.
Edgewater People. New York: Harper and Brothers, 1918. Short stories.
The Best Stories of Mary E. Wilkins. Introduction by H. W. Lanier. New York: Harper and Brothers, 1927.

2. *Articles and Uncollected Short Stories*

Of Mary Wilkins Freeman's approximately two hundred published stories, one hundred fifty have appeared in the volumes of her collected fiction. Almost fifty tales, written for the most part after the decline in her talent began, remain uncollected. Since these, along with some magazine verse and a number of articles, are recorded in the bibliography in Foster's biography *Mary E. Wilkins Freeman*, I have not included most of them here. In general these fugitive pieces contribute nothing to one's understanding of their author. The following brief list contains those of even the slightest significance.

"Pastels in Prose," *Harper's New Monthly*, LXXXVI (December, 1892), 147.

"The Long Arm" (with J. EDGAR CHAMBERLAIN), *The Long Arm and Other Detective Stories* (by others). London: Chapman and Hall Limited, 1895, pp. 1-66.

"Emily Brontë and *Wuthering Heights*," *The World's Great Women Novelists*. Philadelphia: The Book Lovers' Library, [1901], pp. 85-93.

"The Girl Who Wants to Write: Things to Do and Avoid," *Harper's Bazar*, XLVII (June, 1913), 272.

"We Are For France," in *For France*, ed. CHARLES H. TOWNE. Garden City, N.Y.: Doubleday, Page and Company, 1917, p. 336.

"Wake Up, America!," in *America in the War*, ed. LOUIS RAEMAKERS. New York: The Century Company, 1918, p. 34.

Contribution to *My Maiden Effort. Being Personal Confessions of Well-Known American Authors as to Their Literary Beginnings*. Introduction by G. BURGESS. Garden City, N.Y.: Doubleday, Page and Company, 1921, pp. 265-67.

SECONDARY SOURCES

1. *Bibliographies*

BLANCK, J. N. "Mary Wilkins Freeman," *Bibliography of American Literature*, III. New Haven: Yale University Press, 1959. Contains only items published as books or parts of books.

FOSTER, EDWARD. *Mary E. Wilkins Freeman*. New York: Hendricks House, 1956. Contains the most complete listing of Mrs. Freeman's books, articles, uncollected stories, and poems, and of articles about her. The individual pieces in each one of her collections of stories are named.

2. *Biographical and Critical*

All histories of American literature and many anthologies of American literature in general and of the American short story in particular devote space to Mary Wilkins Freeman. To list all of these references, as well as the innumerable newspaper and magazine squibs on Mrs. Freeman, would be wasteful. The selection given below is confined to the most extensive and the most perceptive treatments of her life and work.

BENTZON, TH. [Mme. Thérèse Blanc-Bentzon]. "Un Romancier de la Nouvelle-Angleterre," *Revue des Deux Mondes*, CXXXVI (August 1, 1896), 544-69. Contains a translation of "A New England Nun" and comments on Miss Wilkins as an interpreter of a Calvinist culture.

BROOKS, VAN WYCK. *New England: Indian Summer*. New York: E. P. Dutton and Company, Inc., 1940. General comment on Mrs.

Freeman as a depicter of the economic and spiritual decline of New England.

FOSTER, EDWARD. *Mary E. Wilkins Freeman.* New York: Hendricks House, 1956. The only book-length biography. Excellent coverage of Mrs. Freeman's life and background; contains much critical comment and the most nearly complete bibliography available.

HARTT, ROLLIN LYNDE. "A New England Hill Town," *The Atlantic Monthly*, LXXXIII (April and May, 1899), 561-74; 712-20. A study of cultural decay in back-country New England, with a consideration of Mrs. Freeman as a sensitive and accurate recorder of this decay.

HERRON, I. H. *The Small Town in American Literature.* Durham, N.C.: The Duke University Press, 1939. Discusses Mrs. Freeman as exposer of the meannesses of village life.

[HOWELLS, WILLIAM DEAN]. "Editor's Study," *Harper's New Monthly*, LXXIV (February, 1887), 482-86. Early recognition of Mrs. Freeman as an important new American realist.

HOWELLS, WILLIAM DEAN. *Heroines of Fiction*, II. New York: Harper and Brothers, 1901. Howells discusses the novel *Jane Field* and its heroine.

MACHEN, ARTHUR. *Hieroglyphics.* London: The Unicorn Press, 1960. This volume, first published in 1902, is highly adulatory of Mrs. Freeman's work, which he classifies as *real* literature, *i.e.*, literature of ecstasy.

MACY, JOHN. "The Passing of the Yankee," *The Bookman*, LXXIII (August, 1931), 616-21. Written shortly after Mrs. Freeman's death and in commemoration of the three hundredth anniversary of the founding of Boston, this article discusses the role of Mrs. Freeman and others as historians of a culture now almost extinct.

MATTHIESSEN, F. O. "New England Stories," in *American Writers on American Literature*, ed. JOHN MACY. New York: Horace Liveright, 1931. Contains perceptive comments on Mrs. Freeman's techniques as well as on her significance.

MORE, PAUL ELMER. "Hawthorne: Looking Before and After." *The Shelburne Essays.* Second Series. Boston: Houghton, Mifflin Company, 1905. Places Mrs. Freeman in the tradition of Puritan authors from the Mathers to her own day.

"New England in the Short Story," *The Atlantic Monthly*, LXVII (June, 1891), 845-50. This unsigned article reviews *A New England Nun* along with recently published volumes by Sarah Orne Jewett and Annie Trumbull Slosson. Its analyses of these authors' methods and purposes are perceptive and profound. This is a germinal essay in the study of New England regionalism.

PARRINGTON, VERNON L. *The Beginnings of Critical Realism in America.* New York: Harcourt, Brace and Company, 1930. Parrington compares the writers of rural New England with those of the cities, finding the latter to be less realistic and more enslaved to the genteel tradition. He also attempts a correlation, though inadequate, between Mrs. Freeman's *Pembroke* and Sherwood Anderson's *Winesburg, Ohio.*

PATTEE, FRED LEWIS. *A History of American Literature Since 1870.* New York: The Century Company, 1915. Places Mrs. Freeman in the context of her times in New England and in the nation.

———. *Sidelights on American Literature.* New York: The Century Company, 1922. The chapter "On the Terminal Moraine of New England Puritanism" is the most extensive account and criticism of Mrs. Freeman and her works before 1950; the emphasis is on Mrs. Freeman's fiction as a statement of an expiring outlook and tradition.

QUINN, ARTHUR H. *American Fiction: A Historical Survey.* New York: D. Appleton Century Company, 1936. A brief, factual account of Mrs. Freeman's publications, their realism, and their place in American literature.

ROBINSON, E. A. *Untriangulated Stars,* ed. D. SUTCLIFFE. Cambridge, Mass.: Harvard University Press, 1947. Contains a short, provocative comment by a sensitive New England villager who had read *Pembroke* shortly after its publication.

THOMPSON, CHARLES M. "Miss Wilkins: An Idealist in Masquerade," *The Atlantic Monthly,* LXXXIII (May, 1899), 665-75. A consideration of Mrs. Freeman's themes, which Mr. Thompson finds usually to be some aspect of the Puritan will, and of her style, which he praises for concreteness and simplicity.

WESTBROOK, PERRY D. *Acres of Flint: Writers of Rural New England, 1870-1900.* Washington, D.C.: The Scarecrow Press, 1951. The most extensive study before Edward Foster's biography; a consideration of Mrs. Freeman as one of a group of New England ruralists, including Sarah Orne Jewett, Harriet Beecher Stowe, Celia Thaxter, and others.

WILLIAMS, BLANCHE C. *Our Short Story Writers.* New York: Dodd, Mead and Company, 1926. A review of the types of stories Mrs. Freeman wrote, their themes, their settings, their characters; information as to Mrs. Freeman's writing habits.

WILSON, HAROLD F. *The Hill Country of Northern New England.* New York: Columbia University Press, 1936. A valuable source for social and economic conditions in Mrs. Freeman's New England.

Index